The Baby Dodds Story

*For Jim Cullum
with all good
wishes —
Larry Gara*

The

as told to

Baby Dodds Story

Larry Gara   **Revised Edition**

Louisiana State University Press
Baton Rouge and London

New material copyright © 1992 by Larry Gara
All rights reserved
Manufactured in the United States of America

First published by Contemporary Press in 1959
Louisiana Paperback Edition, 1992

01 00 99 98 97 96 95 94 93 92 1 2 3 4 5

Portions of the Introduction and the text first appeared in *Jazz Journal* (June, 1954, May–December, 1955). Parts of the Introduction also appeared in the December, 1982, issue of the *Mississippi Rag* and are reproduced by permission of the editor-publisher. Portions of Chapters I–III were first published in *Evergreen Review*, I, Nos. 1 and 4.

LIBRARY OF CONGRESS CATALOGING-IN-PUBLICATION DATA

Dodds, Baby, 1894–1959.
    The Baby Dodds story / as told to Larry Gara. — Rev. ed. Louisiana pbk. ed.
       p. cm.
    Discography: p.
    Includes bibliographical references and index.
    ISBN 0-8071-1756-0 (pbk.)
    1. Dodds, Baby, 1894–1959.   2. Jazz musicians—United States—Biography.   I. Gara, Larry.   II. Title.
ML419.D63A3   1992
786.9′165′092—dc20
[B]   91-41646
                                                                                                      CIP
                                                                                                      MN

For Lenna Mae

Contents

PREFACE AND ACKNOWLEDGMENTS *xi*

INTRODUCTION *xiii*

I *New Orleans Beginnings* 1

II *Jazz on The River* 21

III *The Oliver Band* 33

IV *Jazz in Chicago* 50

V *Recording and Broadcasting* 69

VI *Later Years* 85

SELECTED RECORDINGS 97

ADDITIONAL READING 99

INDEX *101*

Illustrations

following page 44

Baby Dodds at Mente's bag factory, 1912

Baby Dodds with Fate Marable's band on the
SS *Sidney, ca.* 1918

Close-up of Baby Dodds with Fate Marable's band

The trombonist Honoré Dutrey

Baby Dodds and his first automobile, *ca.* 1923

Baby Dodds and his drums

King Oliver's Creole Jazz Band, 1923

Mr. and Mrs. Tommy Ladnier and Baby's wife,
Irene, *ca.* 1923

Baby Dodds's favorite picture of himself, 1923

Baby Dodds performing with Jimmie Noone's group, 1942

Baby Dodds recording with Bunk Johnson's band, 1944

Baby Dodds playing the snare drum

Bunk Johnson's band in New York, 1945

Baby Dodds and friends in France, 1948

Baby Dodds performing with Miff Mole's band, 1948

Baby Dodds at the Stuyvesant Casino, *ca.* 1949

Natty Dominique and Baby Dodds, 1954

Baby Dodds with tom tom, 1954

Preface and Acknowledgments

THIS BOOK was first published in 1959 by Contemporary Press, a subsidiary of Contemporary Records in California, which was run by David Stuart and Lester Koenig, now both deceased. Lester Koenig's son, John, held rights to his late father's recording and publishing business and has generously encouraged republication of the book. For the revised edition, I have added an introduction, which highlights certain aspects of the interviews with Baby; a section of suggested additional reading; and a list of selected recordings. In addition, I have changed a few photos in the photo section.

In many ways *The Baby Dodds Story* was a cooperative affair. Many friends aided me along the way. Irene Dodds, who died in 1956, always provided a gracious welcome for Baby's Sunday visitor who invaded her household week after week. Early in the interview process I decided that any errors in Baby's memory should be corrected, since the story was not a memory contest but an account of his life and role in jazz history as he himself saw it. When possible, therefore, changes in names and dates were checked with Baby, and no known error has been allowed to stand in the story. For the checking of names and incidents, Bill Russell's help was invaluable. He not only drew from his own unequaled knowledge of the men and the music but generously permitted me to use some of his materials and photographs. He spent many hours reading and checking the typescript for accuracy. Any errors he did not catch are, of course, my own responsibility, but for the degree of accuracy attained he deserves most of the credit. I am grateful, too, to Dick Allen, who, with his amazing knowledge of New Orleans jazz history, assisted Bill Russell.

Preface and Acknowledgments

The late Dr. Clifford L. Lord, then director of the State Historical Society of Wisconsin, permitted the use of one of the society's tape recorders to record Baby's story. My good friend from high school days, the late Robert Resch, delved into his files of jazz literature to provide material to supplement Baby's story and to supply questions for the interviews.

This edition of *The Baby Dodds Story* is dedicated to my life partner, Lenna Mae Gara, who played an essential role in the work. With minimum complaint she transcribed miles of tape to paper, typed the edited version, and worked on the typescript at every stage. For her help and inspiration there can be no adequate thanks.

Introduction

NEARLY FORTY years have passed since I interviewed Baby Dodds in a series of sessions that led to publication of his autobiography in 1959, shortly after his death. Yet the memory of that time is still vivid in my mind. For me, it was the rarest of privileges and the thrill of a lifetime to hear his important story as he told it to me. Before those interviews, "Baby Dodds" was a name I held in the highest regard because of what Baby had contributed to the music I had loved since my high school days in Reading, Pennsylvania, when I began collecting 78s. It was Baby's drumming that added so much to those great Hot Peppers recordings, and his washboard rhythm that was part of Johnny Dodds's Victor records, which I knew through the Bluebird reissues. I used to listen carefully to those Bunk Johnson Victors, and later Baby's genius was even more in evidence on Bill Russell's American Music recordings of Bunk's band, which reproduced the drum far more clearly than other recordings. So for me the work that went into *The Baby Dodds Story* was not work at all, but sheer pleasure and a refreshing diversion from my other tasks.

In 1953 my other tasks were those of a graduate student in American history at the University of Wisconsin in Madison. My wife, Lenna Mae, and I took a quick trip to Chicago by train one Sunday, and while there we looked up Bill Russell in his North Ashland Street apartment. Subsequently, Bill played a vital role in the whole venture. It was Bill who told us of the upcoming George Lewis concert where I met Baby, then recovering from recent bouts of illness and despondent about his future. It saddened me to learn of his situation, and I got the idea of

Introduction

attempting to record at least part of his story, both to preserve it for the future and to bolster his spirits.

I wrote Baby to request an interview, and then Lenna Mae and I visited him at his 51st Street apartment to discuss the idea further. It was apparent that his health was poor and that any exertion, even an interview, must be limited. Progress on the work would no doubt be painstakingly slow. Before the job was finished, I had spent more than twelve Sunday afternoons with him, each afternoon producing an hour or more of recorded tape. I asked questions about his career and recordings, trying to intrude myself as little as possible. My model, of course, was Alan Lomax' *Mister Jelly Roll,* which had given me the idea in the first place.

As a graduate student with limited funds, I had a number of problems to overcome before I could interview Baby. I had no tape recorder and barely enough money to buy tape. Unfortunately, I recorded the first interviews on cheap, paper-base tape, though I used Scotch plastic-backed metallic tape for most of them. I am happy to report that those ancient tapes still play and that the sound of Baby's voice comes through, muffled though it is by his slurred speech (the result of several strokes) and the poor quality of the tape. To solve the problem of a tape recorder I borrowed an early Webcor from the State Historical Society of Wisconsin. It seemed to weigh a ton as I carried it from a nearby elevated train stop to Baby's apartment. With tape and tape recorder, all I needed was free transportation from Madison to Chicago. I had a friend in graduate school named—believe it or not—Bill Russell, who was a devout member of the Covenanter Presbyterian Church. The nearest Covenanter congregation was in Chicago, so Bill drove there nearly every Sunday. While he attended services, I visited and interviewed Baby. Getting the two Bill Russells together was a joyful footnote to the project.

The Chicago Bill, as I called him, was skeptical of my ability to take on so awesome a responsibility, and his skepticism was well founded. Training in historical research, a love of jazz, and enthusiasm for the project were my only credentials. I knew very little about the history of the music and had not met many jazz musicians. Bill still likes to rib me about the time Baby described a job at the Congress Casino, where he played two novelty numbers, "Tea for Two" and "Dinah," using drumsticks while moving his foot on the tom-toms to vary the pitch. I foolishly asked if his foot was bare. Baby was shocked. Having a bare

Introduction

foot in a public performance was beyond his imagination. Such a naïve question only indicated what I had to learn about the music and Baby's many contributions to it. But what a way to learn! Baby was always patient and cooperative, and by the time we were finished, I had a firsthand account of an important part of classic jazz history.

Getting the material down on tape was only the beginning. Next those tapes had to be transcribed. Lenna Mae agreed to type the interviews, though I'm sure neither of us had any idea of the complexity of such a project. Some of the tapes were not clear, and at times names and words were difficult to understand. Lenna Mae used the same tape recorder I had used, adding a foot pedal to enable her to repeat unclear passages. It was slow going, and nerve-racking enough to wreck a less stable marriage, but we concluded with 320 pages of copy typed in elite type on a battered Royal portable.

We finished the transcription in the summer of 1953, just before we moved to Mexico. There I undertook my first teaching assignment, at Mexico City College. Of course the typescript, along with a thousand records and one change of clothing, went with us. During that school year, in addition to teaching a full load of American history courses and sightseeing in Mexico, I edited *The Baby Dodds Story*. It was literally a scissors-and-paste job, for Baby had discussed similar ideas at different times in the interviews. Sometimes I would ask him to repeat, correct, or elaborate on something he had talked about earlier, so there might be three or four places in the typescript where the same incidents were discussed. I was determined that the story be in Baby's own words, so I limited myself almost entirely to putting sentences together. I did change Baby's wonderful "disremember" to "don't remember," and have regretted it ever since. "Disremember" has special character and should be added to our vocabulary.

This really is Baby's book, and I am still embarrassed when someone refers to me as the author of *The Baby Dodds Story*. My job was strictly one of recording and editing. The book's value is in its authenticity. In my more traditional historical research I had seen how the abolitionists of the 1850s had modified and, in my opinion, ruined the memoirs that fugitive slaves had dictated to them. I was determined not to make the same mistake. There is still unpublished material in the original transcription. Those who have found the book useful have appreciated my approach to recording and editing it. Nothing pleased me more than to

Introduction

read Hugues Panassié's words: "It's a wonderful book, full of life and truth, and it seems to me that I hear Baby Dodds talk."[1]

After the book was transcribed and edited, many questions remained concerning specific incidents and the correct spelling of names. One of the many items that caused a problem was Baby's reference to "plarines" for what we know as pralines. The word came up in connection with Tony Parenti's composition "Praline," which Tony's band recorded with Baby on drums. Baby insisted that the word was "plarine" and that he had never heard the other pronunciation until Tony used it in New York. Bill checked with several older New Orleans musicians, who confirmed what Baby had said. Baby himself also checked the entire typescript for accuracy.

The material Baby put on tape was unique and sometimes surprising. He did not reveal the delightfully uninhibited egotism that Jelly Roll Morton displayed in his famous interview series with Alan Lomax. Nor did he play up the sordid and sensational aspects of the jazz environment as did Mezz Mezzrow in his autobiographical volume. Rather, Baby soberly recorded the ideas and feelings of a man whose life was dedicated to one purpose—the creation of good jazz music. Furthermore, he clearly and unself-consciously listed and analyzed the various ingredients of good New Orleans jazz.

Foremost among Baby's themes was the cooperative or group nature of New Orleans jazz. It was not to be played in such a way that any member of the group was a "standout"; instead, every member was expected to consider the total effect of the music and to do those things that contributed to the good of the whole outfit. Some musicians, Baby complained, never really learned to play together. They never mastered the process of group improvisation.

Throughout Baby's story there also runs the theme of a high degree of craftsmanship. The masters of early New Orleans jazz had high standards. They believed that there was a right way and a wrong way of playing, and until a youngster could prove that he was capable of playing with mature musicians, he was not allowed on the bandstand. Baby recalls vividly the times when members of Kid Ory's band, which included his brother, Johnny Dodds, walked off the bandstand in protest when he sat in on a number by arrangement with Ory's regular drummer. Baby believed that a musician should know not only how to play

[1] Quote in letter to author from David Stuart, March 28, 1960.

Introduction

but also how to take care of his instrument and how to use it to best advantage in all situations. He studied the various drumming techniques used in parades and dances in New Orleans, and he observed carefully the different styles of the drummers in the city. He was always conscious of the sound of his drumming as well as the rhythm, and worked out different techniques for the various outfits with which he played.

Another fundamental of New Orleans jazz that Baby emphasized is the importance of keeping the melody easily discernible at all times. Even Baby's drum carried the melody, for he felt that it was melody people wanted to hear. In their improvisations the New Orleans musicians never lost track of the melody. Moreover, a musician worth his salt could play anything. Baby deplored the preoccupation with certain "standard" jazz numbers, believing that a good musician should be able to take any tune, "put a little jump into it," and turn it into a first-rate jazz number. One of his favorite words for good jazz was "pretty," and he had little sympathy for harsh, loud jazz.

Baby believed that versatility is an absolute essential to a jazz musician. A good drummer must be able to play with any size or kind of outfit. In New Orleans Baby himself played with street parades and dance bands varying in size from just piano and drums to six or seven men. Throughout his musical career Baby played with groups of all sizes, ranging from drums and one other instrument to the Hugh Swift band of fourteen men. He played in brass bands, dance orchestras, show bands, and trios, and even furnished background rhythm for a Merce Cunningham dance recital. For one job Baby played with only Lonnie Johnson's guitar as a melody instrument. Yet Baby took all these experiences as a matter of course. Each one was just another job to him, and as a finished drummer he felt he should be able to do whatever the job called for.

Baby also believed that jazz music should be associated with good spirits, that the music should make people happy. But to produce the right effect it was necessary to have a good feeling in the band. A jazz outfit, he thought, should work in perfect harmony psychologically as well as musically. The wonderful understanding among the musicians in the King Oliver Creole Band and the joy playing together gave them helped them create the music that they nightly produced. Without happiness and good feeling, Baby insisted, a group cannot play the highest type of jazz.

Introduction

New Orleans music was played for dancing, and Baby's measure of achievement was the pleasure felt by folks dancing to it. Crowds that merely stood and listened did not give him the same satisfaction as those who actively participated in the rhythmic experience. Although he played many concerts and jam sessions, Baby always felt that jazz lost an important ingredient when it left the dance halls and became something to which people merely listened.

Of course Baby had a great deal to say about the role of the drum in jazz. To him the drum was almost sacred, and he gave a lot of thought to its function and place. It was no false modesty that made him say that if we could talk to the fellow who invented drums perhaps we would learn something about them. To Baby the drum was "the key to the band," yet drums should really be felt rather than heard. He never beat drums hard or furiously, machine-gun style. His drumming was sharp and clear, without the rumble that drummers often get on the bass drum. Baby believed that the drummer should bring out the best in each of the other players and in the outfit as a whole. He varied his drumming according to the music and the musicians, studying each player in order to provide the background that would make him play the best music he was capable of producing.

Another feature of New Orleans jazz that Baby returned to again and again was relaxation. Frantic, tense jazz was wholly alien to his nature and background. Baby believed that to produce a high-quality jazz the musicians must be relaxed. A good feeling among musicians and dancers enabled him to play without fear or nervous tension. Listening to a New Orleans group play their own brand of music illustrates this point more than any book can reveal. And this is true of all the ideas about music that Baby so aptly put into words.

Although Baby told his story well, there were some things that could be said better by someone else. During one of the sessions Natty Dominique, who then worked at a Chicago airport, joined us at his friend's home and asked to be allowed to comment on Baby Dodds and his drumming. Natty, who had played with Baby and his brother for many years and in numerous Chicago night spots, then recorded a moving tribute to a good friend. His words carry special weight because of Natty's position in the ranks of discriminating jazz musicians:

> Baby Dodds's musical ability is perfect. He reads and plays any

Introduction

kind of music. He's played with me for fourteen years, and with all the different kinds of music which were handed to us Baby read and played his part perfectly. There are many drummers playing with big orchestras nowadays that cannot do that. And Baby studied each player in the bands he played with. There are parts I've had to play on the trumpet that corresponded to Baby's part on the snare drum. And more than once Baby Dodds has contradicted me and told me I didn't play a part correctly. And when I ran over it I saw that he was right, even though I'm a musician myself. I've also seen Baby correct the piano player and other members of the band. Most drummers can't do that, because they're used to a lot of noise.

Baby is not a loud drummer. He doesn't believe in making a lot of noise like some other drummers do. The drummers nowadays believe in beating a bass drum tirelessly. They beat it so fast it doesn't give the tone of the drum a chance to come out. Baby is original. He came out with something that is hard for drummers to get. They haven't got his forty-five-degree angle beat. The drummers nowadays have a short beat. That's bad. You can't get rhythm out of that, it's impossible.

One night at Burt Kelly's Stables I was amazed to find out how softly Baby could drum. The outfit was off the bandstand and a great violinist named Joe Venuti was on the stand. I came upstairs and found that only the violin and drums were playing and the people were dancing, and liked it. And Baby was playing under the violin. The softer the violin would get, the softer Baby would get, and the rhythm was still there. I'll never forget hearing that as long as I live. I had never seen a drummer do anything like that before or since and I said at the time "That boy is great."

Most drummers couldn't do what Baby did because they're used to too much noise. And Baby hasn't got sock cymbals on his drums. That's the worst thing a drummer could have. There's no rhythm in a sock cymbal. No rhythm at all. Just a lot of noise. It's pitiful to see the drummers coming up nowadays, just nothing but noise, no rhythm, and no conception of drumming. And furthermore a real drummer like Baby Dodds will play with sticks, he's not going to bother with brushes. Even a five-year-old child could play with brushes.

And Baby is more than a jazz drummer. Sure, he's the greatest

Introduction

jazz drummer, but during the time I played with him I've seen him play music that was impossible. Some of the other drummers used to come around to the K-Nine Club and to Burt Kelly's Stables and stare at Baby, looking and wondering how he could do it. At the K-Nine Club they threw music at us that was impossible. They had all kinds of different nationality numbers, Spanish, Hungarian, Russian, even Chinese, and Baby Dodds played them all. Because besides being a jazz drummer, Baby Dodds is an accomplished musician.

For me, one of the benefits of the Baby Dodds project was meeting a number of other musicians in the Chicago area. Several times Bill Russell took Baby and me to hear Lee Collins' band, and sometimes Baby sat in for Lee's drummer, Booker Washington. Clarinetist Darnell Howard, who was then selling electronic equipment in Chicago, occasionally visited Baby's apartment. Because of poor health Baby could not do all he wished, and it pained him, though he was still drumming superbly, as his last recordings show. And on Saint Patrick's Day in 1953, when Natty Dominique's fellow airport employees held a dance with mostly New Orleans musicians in the band, Baby worked part of that evening, being spelled off by Jasper Taylor.

Now that Baby and so many he played with are gone, the memories of those visits to Chicago are more precious than ever. There were undoubtedly some lapses of memory and some inaccuracies in his story, but the basic message comes through in the words he used to tell it. It is still amazing to me that I was able to hear all of this from the person whose work as a drummer had thrilled me since my high school days. Baby's story remains one of the best sources of information about early New Orleans jazz, the riverboat era, King Oliver's Creole Jazz Band, and the Chicago jazz of the late 1920s. Moreover, on a personal level, in the process of interviewing Baby and editing the book I learned so much about the value of a high sense of craftsmanship in whatever one undertakes.

It is sad that Baby Dodds did not live to see his book in print, but good to know that this new edition will again make his story available. I believe that my postscript to the 1959 book still has relevance: "Baby Dodds never received the full recognition deserved by one of his genius, yet no serious discussion of jazz drumming can overlook his many con-

Introduction

tributions. His records will always keep memory of him alive. His book, too, will enable people to catch a glimpse of his greatness as a creative artist and as a unique personality. Together, these provide an appropriate tribute to him."

Larry Gara
JUNE, 1991

The Baby Dodds Story

I
New Orleans Beginnings

*"You can't get into a locked house without
a key, and the drum is the key to the band."*

WHEN I WAS just a youngster my mother taught me a poem which I always remembered. It was an ideal which I tried to follow throughout my musical career and it went like this:

> All you do, do with your might
> Because things done by halves
> Are never done right.
> Be the labor great or small,
> Do it well or not at all.

I always worked to improve my drumming and I never drummed just for money. I loved it and I felt that drums have as much music in them as any other instrument. And I think the idea of the guy who invented drums was to have a person beat drums to get something out of them. Quite natural the guy who made them first knew what was supposed to be gotten out of them. But I doubt if anyone knows it today. In my estimation drums should play according to the melody and still keep time. Those to me are the drummer's two specific jobs. Although a drummer can't make a bad note, he provides a very important foundation for the rest of the musicians. You can't get into a locked house without a key, and the drum is the key to the band.

Although I never forgot my mother's lesson, I don't remember too much about her because she died when I was only nine years old. I know that she was a very good-looking, brownskinned woman. She had high cheek bones and a very long Roman nose with a hump in it. I don't recall that she played any musical instrument but she used to sing religious songs with the rest of our family. In school I was always first or second in my class and my mother wanted to send me to Tuskegee to become a doctor. But of course, after she passed away, things turned out differently.[1]

But when I was little I was inspired by music all around. Besides my brother John, who played his clarinet, my father and his brother used to play violin. One of my sisters played a melodian, and my father and sister also used to play harmonicas. My sister used to play some blues and I tried to pick it up. The rest of the family didn't know it because I would get off by myself and try to play different things that my sister played. But I didn't think I was so good with it and I gave it up. My dad also played quills. He took green bamboo reeds and removed the soft spongy material in them. That would leave a clear hole in the reed and then my father would cut them down to about three to six inches, each one a little longer than the other. Then he would put a plug in the top and cut it down, like any other whistle, and he would blow these quills and make very nice music. There was one quill for each note of the scale and he would play almost anything on them. It sounded just like a flute but there was no fingering. I made myself a little set of quills and my father helped me but I didn't make out so well on them. My father was very religious and he only played and sang hymns and sacred music. In fact everybody in the family used to sing. It was the most beautiful quartet you ever heard, to hear that outfit sing. I could sing soprano or tenor and my brother John used to sing real high tenor. And do you know what took it away from him? Clarinet! And do you know what took mine away? Whiskey!

My father worked on a farm part of the time and he was also a handyman for a while. And for a time he worked in a warehouse. He never went to school but he was very good at figures. He was better at arithmetic than I was and he didn't need a pencil and paper to do it.[2] He taught himself to read and write while working in the ware-

[1]Baby tells a story of meeting a schoolmate years later while playing for a medical society dance. His classmate was a doctor and Baby commented on the meeting, "When I saw him I almost went to the floor because I knew how we used to talk about doctors, and he made it, and I didn't. Oh, I felt so small. But he told me, 'I wish I had picked up music!' "

[2]Baby went beyond grammar school and had one year of high. He quit because it was necessary for students in New Orleans to buy their own books when they entered high school. Baby's father told him that if he wanted to buy the books and continue in school he would have to work for them himself. He

house. He was also a first deacon in the Baptist Church. His job was to open the church when the pastor wasn't there and he had to take care of the library. We kids all went to Sunday School, which started at nine-thirty or ten, and we had to stay for the eleven o'clock service which lasted until noon. Since our dad was there we didn't dare leave. And during the service you could hear a pin drop. We didn't dare chew gum or even look up. If we weren't gentlemen on the street, we were gentlemen in church. And church was different from what it is now; there was no hollering or whooping. And they didn't have music in the church, there was only singing.

In those early days I also used to hear classical music. Negroes were not allowed in the places where it was played so I heard it by standing on the outside. Many times I heard symphonies that way. Sometimes we used to stand in the hallway of the Tulane Theatre in New Orleans. One side was an opera house and the other was this theatre and we'd stand in between to hear the music. That is where I learned to like symphony music and I especially loved to hear the flutes. I even wanted to study to be a flute player. I don't see how in the world I ever wanted to play the flute, because there was no field for colored people in classical music. That's why I never took it up. I always liked symphonies and still do. But, being a jazz man, when I hear a symphony I pick out different things which I feel I can use in jazz. And I learned quite a bit from such listening. I used to carry any melody on the snare drums that a band played. I got that idea from listening to symphonic music and also from playing in street parades. They still do that in New Orleans parades, but not as distinctly as they used to.

I began to be interested in becoming a musician when I saw what my brother John was doing. We used to go around to different houses and ask for old bottles which we could sell to the guy that picked up rags and things. Instead of money he'd pay us with candy and whistles. That's where John got a little tin flute. It had only six holes but he was blowing it around, and he would play little things on it. One day my dad asked him what he really would like to play and John said the clarinet. And then my dad got him a clarinet. And the minute

decided to leave school rather than try to work and continue in school at the same time. Concerning this Baby commented, "That's one of the biggest mistakes I've made. I'm sorry today about it."

my brother began to play it he had a perfect tone. That was around 1909, when John was about seventeen and I was only fifteen years old. Of course this interested me. I wanted to get something too and the instrument I wanted was a flute. Since it was out of the question for me to play in a pit orchestra I never got a flute but I still wanted something.

John played his clarinet in the neighborhood and on Sundays he would go and play in parties and he would get all the ice cream and cake. Now I didn't like that. I was the baby in the family and felt I should get the treats. I was especially jealous when John went to different parties and I wasn't even invited. So I finally got an idea. I took a lard can and put holes in the bottom and turned it over and took nails and put holes around the top of it. Then I took some rounds out of my mother's chairs and made drumsticks out of them. Sometimes we used to go in the back yard, to our back place. There was a baseboard and I used to kick my heels against the baseboard and make it sound like a bass drum, using the can as a snare drum. With a clarinet it sounded so good that all the kids in the neighborhood came around to get in on the fun.

By that time I had already got my name "Baby." I was born in New Orleans on Christmas Eve, 1894. Except for my baby sister, Hattie, who was born a few years later, I was the youngest of six children. My name was the same as my father's, Warren. My mother would call "Warren," and I would answer. She'd say, "I'm calling your father." Then she'd say "Warren," and my father would answer, and she'd say, "I'm calling the baby." That's where the Baby came in. My sisters and brothers picked it up and Johnny carried it to school. Of course that did it. I used to get angry about it and I've jumped on many kids and fought them for calling me Baby. When I got out of grammar school the larger girls would call me Baby, and I liked that. I didn't resent the girls using the name but I did the boys. And, of course, anything a person resents is going to happen. After I got into the music business, people found out my name was Baby and it fit perfectly. Baby Dodds is much shorter than Warren and for some reason an alias, or a nickname, will go much farther in life than a real name. And so it was with me, even before I got my first drums.

But I wanted a real drum set. I told my father and he said, "You don't get any drum. How on earth could we stand all that noise! It's bad enough around here now. You'd chase everybody out of the neighborhood." I thought that was very bad. It hurt me and I couldn't understand why he would buy my brother a clarinet and not buy me drums. I knew drums would not cost as much. Of course, in those days, any child who turned out to be a musician was considered no good. As a musician one had to play in places where there was liquor and the chances were he would drink a lot. And I had begun drinking before I started playing music. It wasn't that I had anything on my mind, or drank to drown my troubles, but I used to love the taste of liquor and I always have. Then again we had to play in the tenderloin district. We were looked upon as nobody. Musicians were also very raggedy, and many of them didn't care about their appearance.

But I was determined to get drums and finally my father consented to let me have them if I bought them myself. Well, I didn't mind working because I had helped my father work around the little farm where he worked as handyman. We kids used to help him tend the cows, chickens, ducks, hogs and goats. I used to plant and tend the different vegetables, but I hated to churn the butter which my father made to sell. He wouldn't let me fool around with the cows but I used to feed, curry and clean the horses for him. We were living at Waveland, Mississippi then, so I went to New Orleans and found a job. I was about sixteen years old and got work with a wealthy Jewish family named Levi. My brother's wife worked there as a cook and that's how I got the job. When I went there they asked me if I knew how to wait on tables. I didn't know how and had never waited on a table, but I told them "yes." I worked as a butler and fixed salads, cleaned the rug and took care of the dining room. On Thursdays and Fridays I did the yard work. I worked there about a year and a half and kept that job going until I was able to save up money and buy some secondhand drums. I got only four dollars and six bits a week but managed to save around ten or twelve dollars to buy my first drum. It was a single-head snare drum. I also got some sticks and different little things but it took so long to save up enough to get more drums that I got a job at Mente's bag factory.

At the bag factory I got a dollar and a quarter a day. I did a little bit of everything there. I worked in the drier. We had to hang the sacks on a hook, and after a certain period of time they would go through and come out dry. When they came out I had to count them

The Baby Dodds Story

and put so many in a bundle. There were fifty sacks in a bundle and it was very heavy work. They made sacks of different quality burlap. They used the first class stuff for sugar sacks. Out of others they made coarser grade sugar sacks, coffee sacks, rice sacks and oyster sacks. There were about two hundred and fifty people working at Mente's but quite naturally the colored fellows couldn't get any of the better jobs. They did the heavy work like trucking the bales of burlap in and out, picking up the work off the sewing machines and packing up the bags to go to the press. I worked there for three or four years and did a little bit of everything except the cutting and sewing.

While working there I bought the rest of my drum set one piece at a time. I bought a bass drum, which was a big high thing with ropes like the drums they used in school bands. I had to pull them to tighten and after they were pulled a while the ropes got slick. Then I would let my fingers slide on the rope. It cost me about ten dollars. It was a big, narrow thing and I had no cymbal, foot pedal or anything else. Finally I got a foot pedal, put the set together, and by gimmy, I come to make a noise! I amused the kids in the neighborhood and was real satisfied with myself. Then I added little traps that I needed like a cymbal, wood block, and a ratchet and whistles and things of that sort. I got them all secondhand at a pawn shop but they were as good as new to me. I loved them as much as if they had just come from a factory. It was the hard way and the best way since I knew that I had to take care of them. And I've always tried to take care of my drums. I believe that professional musicians should always try to keep up their instruments. Many drummers don't care how bad their drum sets look. If they can make a dollar on them, they don't worry. I never was that way. I've had some bad looking drums in my day, but it wasn't that the heads had holes in them, or patches, nothing like that. I think that's lazy. If a person makes a living on something and doesn't keep it in top working shape, well, he's just not much good. You can be lazy, but be lazy in some other way, not on the instrument you make your bread on.

The man who was my inspiration when I first started drumming was a fellow named McMurray. I first heard him when I was about fifteen, before I had a chance to get hold of any drums. He was a very tall skinny guy and what a drummer! He played in street parades and in the Robichaux band. When playing for dancing McMurray used a very small snare drum which looked like a banjo, and my inspiration came from his drumming. He used ebony sticks and you would never know that they were so heavy. He played beautiful drums. When he made a roll it sounded like he was tearing paper. It was a marvelous thing. Another wonderful drummer was a Creole fellow named Louis Cottrell. He was very good at examining drums. He could take a snare drum and pick it up and turn it over and examine it to tell if it was any good or not. And he never bought his drums. When the music stores in New Orleans got a new set of drums they would send for Cottrell who would try them out and tell if they were good. He had a very light technique and played both parades and dance band music. He was with the Excelsior Orchestra.

Of course, when I began drumming I soon wanted a teacher because I wanted to know what I was doing, and how to do it. I got a teacher by the name of Dave Perkins. He was very light, like a white fellow, and was a straight man in music. He had an awful big class and taught all kinds of drumming to all colors although he was in a colored neighborhood. But he taught me individually and I paid him by the lesson rather than go in the class. Dave Perkins gave me the rudiments of drumming. And I did all right with him. He gave me a drum pad to use but he didn't want me to use a bass drum. Well, he didn't know I owned one so I practiced there with the pad, and I'd go home at night and execute what I knew on both bass drum and snare. I got along so well, Dave wanted to know if I played anywhere or if I had a bass drum. I told him I didn't have any and he said, "No, I don't want you to touch it." I stayed with him at least a year and after I got so far advanced, and did so well on my bass drum, I went to another teacher.

Meanwhile I had done a lot of street parade work with Bunk Johnson's band. I used to tell them how good I was but still I wanted to go to a teacher some more. I went to a fellow named Walter Brundy. He used to play with Robichaux and was a very good drummer. He was a reading drummer and that's what I wanted to learn—to read music. I didn't get that from Perkins. Brundy taught me the fundamentals of reading music and I found out that everything I had been doing was wrong. He taught me that the right hand was "mammy" and the left "daddy," and I soon learned how to get my two hands working differently. This was, of course, after I mastered having both hands do the same thing. After I got that pretty well, Brundy gave me the two drums to work on. Brundy and Perkins were the only two teachers whom I paid but I got ideas and pointers from lots of others who were playing in New Orleans at that time. I went to Cottrell and learned some more of the rudiments of technique from him. I also got some pointers from a very good drummer whose name was Paps, but we didn't call him Paps, we called him Rabbit. He was with tent shows and I heard that he used to drum for Ma Rainey. I never took lessons from him but learned just by sitting around and looking at him work. For a while he was my favorite drummer. He also played with Armand Piron's five or six piece band and I sat in several times with that outfit. It was a jazz band, but on a higher level. In those days I wasn't reading music so when the time came to read music I had to get up. But they liked my work very much. I got my press roll from Henry Zeno, Henry Martin and Tubby Hall. The guy who used it most effectively was Henry Martin. He played with Kid Ory and it was very effective. It was a pretty hard thing to learn but I worked at it until I got it. Of course I did it in my own way and according to my ability and it never was exactly like someone else's. I used to study the rolls of different drummers at dances and in parades and worked out a long press roll which I preferred to the shorter ones. Tubby Hall's brother, Minor Hall, uses a shorter type press roll today. Where I used three beats, Minor Hall used only one, and of course that makes a different sound.

I also used to listen to some New Orleans drummers who didn't inspire my work. There was Black Benny who was a kind of rowdy fellow. He wasn't a taught drummer but just picked it up. He played so well at it and enjoyed drumming so much that all the fellows liked him from that point and hired him to play. He only played in street bands and there was nothing special about his drumming except that he would always do something to fill in and make some novelty out of it. I heard him when I was very young but his style of drumming was nothing that inspired me.

Of course, a great deal about drumming I had to work out for myself. When you work at something daily, that's yours. I taught myself how to tune my drums and how to put the heads on and tuck them in. The skin was wet when I got them and I learned how to trim the edges and then tuck the heads on. Today they have regular tuckers but when I started we used to tuck them on with a spoon handle. We had to tuck it very tight. And today they don't sell drum heads that you have to wet. They are on the hoop when you buy them. Then we had to put them on the hoop. All those things I had to learn by myself. But when you want to be a drummer, nothing's too hard. And when I was learning I picked up the different drum terms like the mammy and daddy stuff which Brundy taught me. I learned that a biff shot was one abrupt fast lick, a flam is a sixteenth note, a flim-flam is a thirty-second, and a lick is when you just hit the drum. With a lick you just hit it and with a biff you try to make it sound on something, either the rim or anything else solid. The pickup was the first beat and the rudiments are the things we did with a number to be played. It was just different things we did to make the number go and to make the other fellows play. In other words in a calm, ordinary way you push the number and the other musicians too.

When I began playing I soon got a job with Willie Hightower's band, the American Stars. I got it through Robert Smith, the guitar player. I had been working as an ordinary laborer for his father who was a contractor. I started working with gravel and the wheelbarrow and that was pretty tough work. Then I began using the trowel and got paid a much better salary. After Bob found out that I could drum he asked me to come to rehearsal and I got the job with Hightower. With that outfit we played little ice cream party dates and at first all I got was ice cream. I didn't even look for any money and didn't think that I was good enough to get money. I was only about sixteen when I started working with Hightower. It was a very nice little seven-man outfit. Hightower played a trumpet, Roy Palmer played trombone, Wade Whaley played clarinet, and we also had a violin in the group. Hightower was a very nice, even-tempered fellow and I never did see him drink. He played both jazz and straight horn and he'd play one chorus nice and then he would chop it up and play it jazzy.

We began playing dances at lawn parties and fish fries, all outdoors. Through my playing the dates with the Hightower outfit my name began ringing around with different fellows. Roy Palmer, our trombone player, got a job in the tenderloin district, at the Few-clothes Cafe, and he insisted on getting me for a drummer. In the front of the place there was a bar and in the back was a dance floor, cabaret style. There were five of us including a bass player. But Roy let the bass player go and that left only four. Sidney Desvigne played trumpet. He was a very light fellow with light hair and we used to call him "Sheep." Roy Palmer played trombone, Walter Decou, piano, and I played drums. We made some pretty nice music, too. The district was a big field for jazz men. We only made a dollar a night but we would also pass the hat around. Sometimes we took in ten to twenty-five dollars an evening. And that wasn't bad money between the four of us. If somebody asked for a number they would always give you money. Whatever we got we'd bring up and put in the kitty and later divide it among the whole group.

The girls who worked in the district really liked the music and they often sent up for different requests and sent money along. Sometimes they would work along with the band and have the fellows they were with ask for certain numbers. Sometimes they asked the men to give bigger tips for the musicians, too.

In those days we used to play all kinds of numbers. New Orleans is a seaport town and boats would come in from all parts of Europe. Many of the fellows had been on boats for three to five months when they came in and they were glad to find a dance hall and fast women in the district. Then we'd play *Over the Waves* for the sailors and different nationality songs. The men would pay for them because they hadn't heard their native songs in the United States before. We'd also jazz up songs like *In the Shade of the Old Apple Tree*. We used to take waltz tunes and change them into four-four time. And *High Society* we always played as a straight march. Now they play it as a jazz number. And the whole point of that number is the clarinet solo. It was Picou's number and he did wonderfully on it. We played what was later called ragtime but was then called syncopation. It was picked up off Scott Joplin. It was called syncopation before I even started playing. And we always stressed the melody. That's the secret of jazz music, to carry the melody at all times. The melody is supposed to be heard distinctly, carried by one specific instrument, the trumpet, trombone, clarinet or violin.

On New Orleans dance dates we also had to play mazurkas, quadrilles, polkas, and schottisches. There were certain halls in New Orleans where you had to play all those things. Some of the Creole people went only for that music. If you couldn't play them you just didn't get the job.

Of course we also played the blues. Some of the guys would come in and drink with women and they would be blue about something, and they would ask us to play the blues. The blues that were popular were the *Memphis Blues,* the *St. Louis Blues,* and *Careless Love. Bucket Got a Hole In It* was also a blues type of number and *Ace in the Hole* was another. The blues were played in New Orleans in the early days very, very slow, and not like today, but in a Spanish rhythm.

After I left the Fewclothes outfit I worked for a piano player named Manuel Manetta, who also played in the district. The place was called the Casino. It was a little uppity place that had about five or six men in the band. It had been known as the Villa Cafe but some killing had gone on there and the owner changed the name to the Casino. Before long I left the district and went back to Hightower. I was glad to get away from the district anyway. I didn't like that sort of life. Furthermore, I had a girl in the district who wanted to cut my throat.

In the meantime Hightower got a regular job playing at St. Catherine's Hall, which was a Catholic school. Ory's band had been playing there but he gave up the job and when Hightower found out about it he spoke to the priest in charge. The school used to give dances every Friday and Sunday. We didn't get both days but we got the Sunday dates. When I first went there I didn't even think about whether I was going to get paid or not. I wasn't particular and I was especially excited about the work because my brother John had played in the same place with Ory. All I wanted to do was to get a chance to play where my brother used to play. And we made very good and kept up those Sunday dances for a long time. I played with the American Stars off and on for several years.

It was when I was working with Willie Hightower's outfit that I first realized how important drums were to a band. Sometimes when I had to go out and happened to hear the group start to play, I could feel that something was missing. And the greatest satisfaction of my entire musical career was knowing that I belonged there. Without the drum there was something lacking. No instrument can take the drum's place. With all the outfits I played, I felt that I was just as essential in the outfit as any other instrument in it. I knew I had to do my part. I had to beat drums because nothing else answers. Without my filling in my part it would mean a difference. Of course, I never worked any place where I felt I was the whole thing. I felt that all the other instruments were needed too. No one can do anything by himself. If there are more than two it's a group and I feel that all members are essential. In playing music I always felt that I was part of the group and not an individual performer.

When I first started playing in New Orleans I heard a lot of good jazz musicians. There were Buddy Petit, Joe Johnson, George Larroque and Andrew Kimball, trumpet players, and Frankie Duson, trombone player. There was also a tall dark fellow by the name of Eddie Jackson who used to play a very good tuba. He could play both sweet and hot. But in those days they only used tubas in street parades, never in dances. Sometimes I used to go out to Lincoln Park where both Buddy Bolden and John Robichaux were playing. Robichaux had a sweet band and they would sometimes play classics in swing. Those days they didn't call it jazz, but they called it swing. Robichaux played in a closed-in place like a pavilion and the better class people came to hear his band. Bolden had a band which played in an open place with only a roof over it. The sporting class of people would go to hear Bolden, but both bands played for dancing and the people went to dance, not just to listen. We used to call it a honky tonk where Bolden played and his men were the bums. I heard Bolden play but I can't remember anything about him or the music. He was one of the big guys of the day. Those days they had four or five trumpet men that were very good but Bolden was supposed to be king of them all. I also heard Picou play clarinet when I was little and he was really great. George Baquet was another guy playing clarinet who was just about as great as Picou. And of course, besides hearing jazz music played for dancing, I heard jazz in all the New Orleans parades. I also knew Jelly Roll Morton from the time I was a kid, and the great pianist, Tony Jackson. I used to work in the place he worked but that group of men was older and I never got close to them. To even get in a conversation with them I had to buy them a lot of drinks or just pass by and take what I could get and go in. In those days a beginner wasn't allowed to be with a bunch of men that played such a high class of music. They wouldn't have anything to do with us.

I played with Big Eye Louis Nelson in different bands and at different times. He used to play clarinet with the Duson band, not as a regular player, but just now and then. He was a very determined fellow, especially on the young musicians just starting up. He'd show a youngster all he knew but he had a very glum disposition. He knew he had to be stern with those of us who were learning. He didn't kid around much and we never got to be close friends. He lived downtown, and I lived uptown. He was on the north side of town and I lived on the south side. In other words, he was a Creole and lived in the French part of town. Canal Street was the dividing line and the people from the different sections didn't mix. The musicians mixed only if you were good enough. But at one time the Creole fellows thought the uptown musicians weren't good enough to play with them, because most of the uptown musicians didn't read music. Everybody in the French part of town read music. Then too, the Creole people in New Orleans were very high strung. Most of them had a little better education and it seems as though they had a little more money. When they went into music they were given money to get a teacher and they would learn music from the start. My brother and I were really exceptions in that we both got teachers and became reading musicians.

Of course in those days the instrumentation was different. When I first started out they had no piano. They mostly used bass viol, guitar, clarinet, trumpet, trombone and drums. The guitar carried only rhythm in the bands. Actually you have a much sweeter jazz band when you have a guitar and no piano. In that way the drums couldn't outplay the other guys, because the drummer had to keep in touch with the guitar. The guitar is not a harsh instrument but a very melodious one. When the piano came in it was harsher and louder than the guitar, although in my time we had some guitar players that were awful loud. There were Johnny St. Cyr, Brock Mumford and Lorenzo Stall. Later they switched to banjo. I think the first band to switch was Frankie Duson. They made the change because the banjo was a novelty. And they used two types of banjo, the regulation and the tenor.

In many places they had nothing but just piano and drums. In fact, on one occasion, I had to play a whole evening with nothing but drums and trombone. That was with Jack Carey. We had a date to play up town in what they called the Irish Channel. The Irish people liked the colored music and they hired Jack Carey's outfit. He had no regular drummer but would hire individuals for different dates, and that time he wanted me to play with the group. It had rained in the afternoon and a lot of fellows failed to appear at the dance. Only Jack Carey and I showed up with our drums and trombone. Well, those Irishmen were very tough on colored fellows and we wanted to avoid a misunderstanding. We knew if we played the best we could they'd be satisfied. After waiting a half hour we noticed that a lot of the Irish fellows were getting drunker and we knew what would happen if the music didn't start soon. So we began to play that way and played the whole dance through. I think it sounded all right, too. Carey played a rough, tailgate style trombone and they liked it very much. He carried the melody and quite natural I was there with the time, so there was nothing to worry about. We both had to work very hard though, because on the drums I had to do everything to fill in, to make it sound like something. We knew we couldn't sound like a full band, but they danced to it and there was no trouble.

Jack Carey was a wild and quick tempered fellow. He was older than his brother Mutt, who played trumpet. Sometimes he was quite loud and boisterous. Mutt was very quiet. Jack wanted to have things perfect but when he tried to explain something carefully he couldn't do it, and then he would get all upset. Mutt had more of an ability to explain things than Jack. They were different in all ways. Mutt was a very light fellow and Jack had a dark skin. Mutt was always kidding and joking and I never saw him really angry. And *Tiger Rag* they used to call *Play, Jack Carey*. The part where they say "hold that tiger," Jack Carey would make on the trombone and they used to say "Jack Carey, Jack Carey!" Everybody played it that way saying "Jack Carey" instead of "hold that tiger."

While I was playing around with different outfits my brother was established and playing with Kid Ory's band. He had studied clarinet under different fellows. One was Papa Tio, the old man Lorenzo, and Charlie McCurdy was another one. They were both straight musicians, not jazz men. And when John came along, he came along against Sidney Bechet. That meant he really had to fight. John got the job with Ory through Pops Foster. Foster was with the Ory band and they were using Wade Whaley on clarinet. Pops Foster happened to come by the house and hear John's clarinet. He stopped on the sidewalk and knocked on the door and asked my brother if he wanted to join a band. My brother said "yes" and Pops Foster told Ory and everybody he had a pretty clarinet player he would like them to hear. They had a rehearsal of some sort and John joined Ory, and he played with him a number of years.

Sometimes I would go around to dances in New Orleans where my brother was playing with Ory. I used to go to the drummer, Henry Martin, and get him to let me drum. He would get up and I would sit down in the band. And then the band fellows would look around and see it wasn't the same style of drumming. My brother and Ory and the others didn't think that I was capable or good enough to play in that band, and they'd walk off the stand one by one, until all the fellows were off but the bass player and me. The bass player was Eddie Garland, and the next thing he would be laying the bass down, and I'd know there was nothing for me to do but get down. And when I'd get down the band would all come back again. It was very embarrassing. They pulled that quite a few times, made me feel awfully bad. I was determined, though. I felt as though a baby must crawl before it can walk, and I felt that I wasn't quite ready to walk yet and just took it for granted. And for encouragement I would go around and do the same thing all over again. That gave me ambition to learn. I was trying to play with someone who was capable of playing. And many times later I returned the compliment. But I never did get over the feeling I had towards Ory. Later I played with him on the West Coast but I never got close enough to Ory to know him. It's a respect that I gave him that I perhaps wouldn't give anyone else.

The musicians of those days were remarkable men. When the leader of an orchestra would hire a man, there was no jealousy in the gang. Everybody took him in as a brother, and he was treated accordingly. If a fellow came to work with anything, even a sandwich or an orange, the new man would be offered a piece of it. That's the way they were. They believed in harmony. That's how they played music, in harmony. And that's the way the fellows were, those old-timers. And I was young and I had to give them a lot of respect. If those men would happen to like you enough to pick you up, they would either make a musician out of you, or you wouldn't be any musician. In their way, they were rough, but in a way they weren't rough. Everything they told you they would make you do for your own benefit. But I used to try to drum and I'd drum my best and they knew I was doing my best and they all said the same thing. They said, "Someday he's going to be a good drummer because he pays attention. He wants to learn." And I did.

But while I was learning I kept playing and I left the American Stars to join Frankie Duson's Eagle Band. Duson was a very high strung, good looking fellow. He was part Indian and had a brown skin but reddish complexion. He had a high nose with a lump in the middle—real Indian nose—and very long curly hair. He played tailgate trombone, something like Ory, but a little smoother and with a bit more polish. Bunk Johnson played trumpet in that outfit. The little fellow that was the drummer, Henry Zeno, got sick and died, practically overnight. He ate raw oysters and drank whiskey, and it killed him. I had built such a reputation around New Orleans that they said "Let's get Babe." Then that made me play the street parades, too. It was the first time I played them. Different social clubs in the city would hire our band. They would have bands to turn out with a parade or for some other function. Sometimes it was anniversaries or social occasions and sometimes the funeral of a member. With the brass band I only had one drum, the snare drum. Someone else played the bass drum. We also played for dancing with the Duson band but it was a bigger outfit when we played parades.

There was a traditional line-up for the New Orleans parades. The trombones were always first. Behind the trombones would be the heavy instruments, like bass, tubas, and baritones. Then behind them were the altos, two or three alto horns, and behind them were the clarinets. It was very good if there were two. Usually it was only one, an E flat. Then behind the clarinet would come the trumpets, always two or three, and they came next. Bringing up the rear would come the drums, only two, a bass drum and a snare drum. That was for balance. For funeral marches the snare drum is muffled by pulling the snares off. When the snares are off it's the same as a tom-tom. But you don't muffle drums with parades, or going back from the cemetery. At the most there were eleven or twelve men in the whole brass band. I never noticed what the people who followed the bands did because my attention was all on my music. Maybe I'd cast my eye and perhaps see something funny, but it was only a minute and then right back to my music. In the parades they had horses and men with sashes and the like, but the music was all I was interested in.

Sometimes the groups would have several bands in a parade. Then the main band had to start first and finish last and all the other bands had to go through this leading band at the end of the parade. Of course the head band would always be the best. And it was one of the most exciting things I ever did to play music and go through another band that was playing. The main band was lined up on both sides and we had to go between them and keep playing. I remember the first time it happened. I don't remember who was drumming in the main band but I think it was Ernest Trepagnier who was beating bass drum. The snare I don't remember. But my snare drum was a four-inch drum, and this fellow had a six-inch snare drum. When we got going through I couldn't hear my drumming anymore so I didn't know what I was doing. And I picked up with the other drummer who was playing six-eight in contrast to the two-four time we had been playing. I should have displaced the other fellow's drumming with concentrating on what I was doing but that time I heard the other guy's part and not my own, and of course we were playing altogether different numbers. But it's those experiences which make you know what music is, and it's the hard way of learning.

I played many a funeral with brass bands in New Orleans. The first time I ever heard the number *Didn't He Ramble* was in a street parade after the burial of a corpse. He had been a member of a secret society and so they hired a band to play for his funeral. He was the type of fellow who would go out and have a good time, and cheat on his wife. In other words he was the type of person who would throw a brick and hide his head. But when he came home he was a saint. And so they made this number. They claim that Buddy Bolden made it but I don't know. If the musicians found out that this was the kind of man who was being buried they would play this song. It meant a lot of things that weren't just out and spoken.

Of course we played other numbers coming back from funerals. We'd play the same popular numbers that we used to play with dance bands. And the purpose was this: As the family and people went to the graveyard to bury one of their loved ones, we'd play a funeral march. It was pretty sad, and it put a feeling of weeping in their hearts and minds and when they left there we didn't want them to hear that going home. It became a tradition to play jazzy numbers going back to make the relatives and friends cast off their sadness. And the people along the streets used to dance to the music. I used to follow those parades myself, long before I ever thought of becoming a drummer. The jazz played after New Orleans funerals didn't show any lack of respect for the person being buried. It rather showed their people that we wanted them to be happy.

On other occasions we played jazz on the streets to advertise dances and lawn parties. Private individuals used to sponsor these parties and they were held in outdoor pavilions rather than dance halls. They'd have just a tarpaulin or tent over the top to keep the night air off, and sometimes they would have a tarpaulin stretched out on the ground for the people to dance on. Sometimes they'd dance on the natural ground. They'd smooth it off nice. And the only advertising they had would be to get the band on a wagon and put a couple of posters on the side. We would sit there and go from block to block or corner to corner, and play. Of course when the people came out to hear the band they would see the posters. I used to play on such wagons when I first started with the American Stars and later with Frankie Duson's Eagle Band, and still later with Celestin. For a fact, all the bands used to advertise that way. We would start out about two o'clock in the afternoon and wouldn't get back till around five.

When some other outfit was also advertising and we met each other along the street in those wagons it used to make it very interesting. The guys would put the wheels together and tie them so the band that got outplayed could not run away. That made us stay right there and fight it out. And we used to draw quite a crowd of people in the street that way. We didn't call them cutting contests, but if we said that a band cut you on the street, that meant they outplayed you. And that was passed along through jokes. We talked about who got chased, or which band "fixed them guys," and that sort of talk.

I'll never forget one time when we were stopped on the streets. I was playing with Jack Carey on that occasion. I didn't belong to the band but they used to get me to play. Jack Carey played trombone, his brother Mutt, cornet, and Carey's nephew named Zeb, clarinet, and we ran across Ory's band. Quite natural the Ory band had the best of it all. Besides Ory, my brother was in that band, and Joe Oliver. Of course we didn't have a chance, but we had to stay there. When we played a number there wouldn't be much applause, but when Ory played we would hear a lot of people whistling and applauding. When we heard that, quite naturally our courage went down and we wanted to get away. But the wheels were tied together. It lasted about an hour and a half or two hours and it was very discouraging. I wasn't so good. I was just starting and Ory's drummer, Henry Martin, was a finished musician, but those things are what made us want to become good musicians because it made us know what we had to do better.

But I improved as time went on and I left the Duson band to join Sonny Celestin's outfit. Sonny had heard that I was young but wanted to learn and he hired me. We played at a place called Jack Sheehan's Roadhouse. It was a cabaret style place. They'd sell setups and glasses, and people could either bring their own whiskey or buy it there. It was prohibition but they sold whiskey anyway because it was on the outskirts of New Orleans. They also had roulette wheels for gambling and some card games. We played only for dancing and there were six of us in the outfit: Celestin on trumpet, Bebé Ridgley, trombone, Zutty Singleton's uncle Willie Bontemps, played bass and guitar, and Lorenzo Tio, clarinet. It was mostly a reading band. Only two didn't read music. And we had a girl piano player. She was a very good looking, light colored girl named Emma Barrett. She had big eyes; we used to call her "Eyes." She was a very thin girl but oh my God, she could play nice piano. She played like any man.

They were all good musicians. Celestin played very sweet horn. He never was much of a jazz man on horn. He played mostly straight. Still, with everybody else jazzing and him playing straight, it sounded awfully good. Bebé Ridgley was also a very nice guy who played nice trombone. His playing wasn't rough but sweet, more like Honoré Dutrey's. Willie Bontemps was a very big fellow who weighed two hundred pounds or more. He suffered from asthma and had to use an atomizer. Lorenzo Tio was more of a Mexican type fellow. He was Creole, very tall with very straight black hair. He was a very easygoing fellow and he used to love to play. He had a cute little joke which he liked to play on Sonny. Celestin was very sleepy; we used to say he was lazy, but he was just a sleepyhead. After playing he'd put his horn down in his lap and go to sleep. Then for a trick Tio would take some newspaper, tie it to the back of Sonny's chair, and set fire to it. One night Celestin jumped up and almost ran out of the place. He was very angry with Lorenzo, and Tio had to hide from him for about half an hour until he got his temper down. It's the only time I've ever seen Celestin really mad. He was pretty sore but later he took it as a joke, too.

When I was with Celestin we played more pop numbers than when I was in the Duson Band. We didn't call them pop numbers though, we called them classical numbers. That is, not the rowdy type, such as blues, nothing like that. The customers at Jack Sheehan's were all white and the blues would not have been appreciated. It wouldn't be any use to play them. One of the main numbers which we played was *Liza Jane*. I used to sing that and Sonny would put his horn in his lap and start clapping in time. But before he got the time he'd be going asleep. I'd have to say "Come on Sonny!" and then he'd wake up and join in the number again. Later, after I left the band, Sonny sang the number himself and then all the fellows joined in. Before that I don't think Celestin knew he could sing.

It was at Jack Sheehan's that I worked out my shimmy beat. It was wartime, around 1918. One night a French soldier came in. When he heard the music he couldn't dance to it, but he just started to shake all over. That's the way it affected me. I saw him do it and I did it, too. The people got such a kick out of seeing me shaking like him that they all came around and watched. Then when I saw that it caused such a big sensation and brought credit to myself and my drumming, I continued it. I used to shimmy at the same time I used my press roll and a full beat. It was perfect. I slapped my left foot, the right foot was busy, and it worked very nicely. I used it ever since that time and it became a specialty with me.

Although I didn't realize it at the time, my days of playing in New Orleans were coming to an end. Before long I joined the Fate Marable band and played on the riverboats, and from there I went to the West Coast and Chicago with King Oliver. But it was in New Orleans that I got my start.

II
Jazz on The River

"We played strictly by music. And music is not so hard if your get with a bunch that's playing together."

IT WAS around the latter part of 1918 when Pops Foster got me the job playing on the riverboat. I had been playing with Sonny Celestin's band and left that outfit to work on the boat. Pops also wanted to get Louis Armstrong. He figured that I could do more with Louis than he could and he asked me to get him for the band. Louis was playing with the Ory band. So was my brother, John. So I was fighting to get Louis on the boat, and my brother was fighting to make him stay with Ory. Finally, I won out. It was a big job but I made it and we had Louis with us on the boat. Louis and I stayed on the boats from the fall of 1918 until September of 1921.

The boats belonged to the Streckfus line. They had jazz bands for dancing on all their boats. At first I played on the steamer *Sidney*, working out of St. Louis in the summer, and out of New Orleans for seven winter months. After my first year on the boat they brought the steamer *St. Paul* out of dry dock. It was a much larger boat. The *Sidney* held only about eight hundred but the *St. Paul* had a capacity of thirty-five hundred. After that they used the *Sidney* in New Orleans only. I played on four boats in all: the *Sidney*, the *St. Paul*, the *J.S.* and the *Capitol*. Later they added the *President*. I was on that boat when it came out of dry dock but I didn't work on it. We would leave New Orleans around the fifteenth of May and head up the river for St. Louis. We played in St. Louis from about the fifteenth of June until the fifteenth of September, but we also took trips out of some towns farther up the river. We went all the way up to St. Paul and stopped in Davenport, Dubuque and Keokuk, Iowa, LaCrosse, Wisconsin and Red Wing, Minnesota on the way.

In St. Louis they used to give colored excursions every Monday night. It was one of the most wonderful things you've ever seen carried on. The boat was packed and we got such a kick out of it because it gave us a free kind of sensation for working. We worked all the week for white people and this one night we could work for colored. It gave us an altogether different sensation because we were free to talk to people and the people could talk to us, and that's a great deal in playing music. We were less tense because it was our own people. I especially loved it because I made a big sensation with my shimmy beat. I used to shimmy and drum at the same time, shake all over. The colored people had never seen anything like that. I used to have a bunch around me backed up five or six deep; and Louis Armstrong would have a bunch five or six deep backed up around him. It was a wonderful thing, and we were the two sensational men on the boat, Louis and I.

We certainly enjoyed working on the boats and we were paid well, too. We were getting fifty dollars a week and five dollars a week bonus. That was to force us to stay on the whole season; we wouldn't receive the bonus until the season was over. We also got our room and board on the boat. The bunks were very comfortable but we stayed down in the hold. However it was very clean and nice. The band and the roustabouts were the only colored people on board. The dozen of us in the Marable Band all ate at a separate table. Some of the fellows thought the food was good but I didn't think so. We had mostly stews, salads, wieners and things like that. That's nothing to feed anybody. When we got to St. Louis we preferred to board ourselves rather than stay on the boat and eat that food.

And they were pretty strict about what we did, too. After we left New Orleans to go up the river, we had nothing to do but be on the boat. We ate and slept right on the boat. Every time we got off work we went right back down in the hold and went to sleep, or did what we wanted to at night: play cards, or shoot craps, or something. There was nobody to win money from except one another. When we went out at night there was a curfew. And if we weren't there at a certain time we didn't get on the boat. We got off work at eleven and we could leave the boat until curfew, which was about one-thirty.

The bosses demanded discipline. I remember once when I was in Keokuk, Iowa I got into a humbug. We all piled off the boat one day and I got so drunk I couldn't see. They were using this homemade beer, they used to call it "bust-head" in Keokuk, and I came back to the boat so drunk with the stuff that I just couldn't walk up the gangplank. They tied me to a post and one of the bosses said I should have been horsewhipped. I said "Yeah? I'll bet it would be the worst horsewhipping you ever saw if you'd let me alive when you got through." They were kind of shy of me. I didn't care about anything in those days so maybe I would have done something, I don't know.

But my heart was in my music, and that was some of the sweetest music I ever played. It was a wonderful outfit. Besides the standard jazz and popular numbers we played classical numbers and also played for ordinary singing. The Marable Band was the first big band that I worked with. We had about a dozen men. It was a pleasure to work with that bunch of men. We didn't have to work hard. Of course, we worked hard but we didn't have to. We played strictly by music. And music is not so hard if you get with a bunch that's playing together. But it's an awful strain to play jazz with one fellow going this way and another fellow going another. That makes for hard work. It's like anything else. If you run an automobile and the gears are meshing easy you can run it pretty fast. But if the gears are meshing badly, they're going to hit each other. It's the same thing with music. Regardless of what the number is, if everybody's together, and if everybody knows his business, when the notes are joined they'll come out even. The music would sound so pretty, especially on the water. And the mellophone set the band off and gave it a different tone from any other band I worked with. It was something great to hear. Everybody was so congenial, too. We had so much harmony in that band.[1]

The leader, Fate Marable, was a very light-colored man with red hair. He was a pretty stern fellow who kept strict order. Marable had worked for Streckfus so long, and he looked so white, that people used to say he was Streckfus' son. He was the best calliope player I ever heard. I've heard them played in the circus but no one could play like that guy. He had a calliope on top of the boat which he used to

---

[1]When asked how the Marable band compared with the Oliver band Baby said: "Oh, it was a different type. You see the Oliver band was a real jazz band. They played nothing but jazz music. But with the band on the boat we played some semi-classics and numbers like that."

play alone. Three decks down, where the band played, he had a little electric chimes, which worked just like a calliope. He played mostly piano with the band but he would use the chimes just to make the band sound a little different at times.

There were some other wonderful musicians in the riverboat band besides Fate Marable. There was Joe Howard who was a very even-tempered nice-going fellow. He would try to tell you everything right if he possibly could and would show us anything that he could to improve the group. But he would get angry with himself sometimes and we could see the different expressions on his face. He would never bother anybody though. He helped Louis a great deal with the mastering of musical ability.

Davy Jones, who played mellophone, was another easy-tempered fellow who didn't drink at all. His musical ability was also very high and he would show anyone all he knew. And his mellophone gave the band a sound you don't often hear. He played it with the bell of the horn in his lap. Other players turned it up. The sound from the bell would come in his lap. It muffled the tone and made it sound so beautiful.

Sam Dutrey was a fine fellow but he was very high strung. However, he and I used to get along beautifully. We were close friends, just as his brother, Honoré, was my best friend in the Oliver outfit later. He also tried to get me to save some of my money.

Of course, Louis was also with us. I remember, when he first came on the boat, he didn't have a horn. And in Davenport, Iowa, Bix Beiderbecke and some of the other white musicians came on the boat to listen and talk to the different musicians. Louis told Bix he didn't have a horn, so Bix said, "Well, meet me when I go out and I'll see if I can get you a horn." And Bix took him out afterwards and helped him pick out a horn.

There's a story about Louis and some of the others buying bootleg liquor on the boat. It was during prohibition time and we were glad to get even a drink of liquor, especially good liquor. One day a fellow came on the boat with a suitcase out of which he pulled a bottle. We all had a taste of it and we asked him how much he wanted. He said, "Twenty-five dollars a quart." We knew whiskey was tough to get so we all said "yes." He said he would have to come back and bring it to the dock at a certain time and we planned a time to have it on our intermission so we could meet him. When he came during intermission we were waiting. I don't know what happened but I ducked out of it and decided I didn't want any. Then Fate borrowed the twenty-five I had put in. He and Louis had earlier paid for one quart each so that meant the fellow got seventy-five dollars. But when we got back on the boat we found out there was nothing in the suitcase but three bricks. Naturally, we lost all of the money and never saw the fellow again. But we had a big laugh and kidded Louis and Fate a long while about it. It was a real laugh for me, because even though my money went, I had backed out of it after I had been one of the instigators. And of course everybody knew I loved whiskey.

But with all our joking we never got away from the music and we always tried to work out new ideas. Louis was especially versatile. Once Streckfus bought some trick instruments for the different people in the band. He bought Louis a slide trumpet and me a slide whistle and different little trinkets that were to go with my drums. That's what they call traps. A snare drum isn't a trap drum. Rather traps are such things as blocks, triangles, slide whistles, horns, tambourines, cocoa blocks and things like that. In those days nobody handled these traps but the drummers. And if you couldn't handle the traps you didn't get a job. Well, Streckfus bought this slide whistle for me but I didn't even look at it. Louis did. He played it and years later he used it sometimes with the Oliver band. Joe wanted him to make a recording with it so he took the whistle along to a recording session and played it on the Oliver record of *Sobbin' Blues*.

Louis also had a lot to do with the popularizing of jazz words. He used certain expressions on the riverboats, like "Come on, you cats," and "Look out, there, Pops," and the like. These were his own ideas. I had never heard such words as "jive" and "cat" and "scat" used in New Orleans. There was one exception, however, which you don't hear now. We used to call white musicians "alligators." That was the way we'd describe them when they'd come around and we were playing something that we didn't want them to catch on to. We'd say "watch out, there's an alligator!" But these other terms Louis had a lot to do with.

I think it was on the riverboat where Louis developed his gravel voice. He had a cold all the time and we used to kid him around, laughing and joking. Once he took a whole course of Scott's Emulsion. It cleaned him out perfectly and then he had to get plenty of rest on the boat since there was no special place to go. He got rid of the cold but the voice had developed like that and he's been like that ever since.

Louis learned a lot about music from Joe Howard on the boats, and I also learned a great deal about music during that time. I knew how to spell when reading music but I didn't know how to read well and fast. We had loads of fun and had an hour and a half or two-hour rehearsal almost every day, all new music. That's why we learned to be such good readers. New music every day, and the same music we rehearsed in the day we played at night. And we had to be perfect with it. There were three Streckfus brothers, and they were all musicians. I think two of them played piano and one, violin. And they made Fate demand frequent rehearsals of the band. It was wonderful for me and everyone else concerned. It made us tidy up our music, it made our eyes fast and it made us fast on our instruments. That was the first place I learned what "time" was. They would hold a metronome on me, and a stop clock, and I wouldn't know anything about it. I had to be a very strict time keeper in those days. I used to listen to everybody in the group and try to give each one what he wanted. Nobody tried to outplay the other fellow. We all played together, and Louis was the only one who took solos in the Marable Band.

It was on the riverboat that I began using the rims instead of the woodblocks. I don't remember the number but on one that called for woodblocks I used the rims of the bass drum instead. And it sounded so pretty. The woodblock gave a loud sound, and I substituted the shell of the drums, and it sounded so soothing and soft. Sometimes I used faster beats on the rims. Then again, when it was a slow number, I'd do it in triplets. It was pretty and soft, and still it would make the number lively. I worked out these things by myself on the boat because I knew I had to make good. That's also where I learned to be so tough on drumming. At that time I could sit down and drum a pretty long time.

On the boat I also worked out the technique of hitting the cymbal with the sticks. I worked that out around 1919. Now everybody's using it, but it came from me on the riverboat. There was a side cymbal that used to be on the drum. I took that off and then it was a straight boom, boom, boom. Of course, I still used the two cymbals on top of the bass drum. There was a regular cymbal and a Chinese cymbal. The Chinese cymbal had a different tone. We all used it in those days but Ray Bauduc's about the only one I know who uses it now.

It was about the same time that I helped cause the sock cymbals to be made. I was in St. Louis working on the steamboat and William Ludwig, the drum manufacturer, came on the boat for a ride. He was very interested in my drumming. I used to stomp my left foot, long before other drummers did, and Ludwig asked me if I could stomp my toe instead of my heel. I told him "I think so." For a fact I thought nothing of it. So he measured my foot on a piece of paper and the space where I would have it and where it would sit and he made a sock cymbal. Two cymbals were set up and a foot pedal with them. One day he brought one along for me to try. It wasn't any good, so he brought another raised up about nine inches higher. Well, I had just taken the cymbal off the bass drum because I didn't want to hear that tinny sound any more and I didn't like the sock cymbal either. I didn't like any part of them and I still don't. Now it's a big novelty for drummers. Some drummers can't drum without them. I can't drum with them.

However, I knew that if it made a success I wouldn't get a dime so I didn't want any part of it. I was glad to help at first but I didn't want any part in demonstrating it. He wanted me to be one of the founders of it. It was to be a Baby Dodds pattern. But I wouldn't have it. If he made good on it, he made good. And of course he did.

But I made good, too, with my drumming and there's a story about my teacher Brundy which shows the progress I made. We were working on the steamer *St. Paul* and there was another excursion boat, the *J.S.*, which was a sister to the *St. Paul*. The only difference between the two boats was that the *St. Paul* was a flat-bottomed boat and the *J.S.* was a keel-bottomed boat. After we had made such a hit in St. Louis Streckfus wanted to get another colored band for the *J.S.* They got an outfit from New Orleans and Brundy was in it. After he had played a while Streckfus told him, "You come over on the steamer *St. Paul* and listen to that drummer." When Brundy came on and I saw who it was, I told Streckfus, "My God, I can't do no drumming. This fellow's my teacher. He taught me how to drum." He said, "It doesn't matter if he did, you can drum better than he can." And

The Baby Dodds Story

Streckfus told him so. Brundy replied, "If my scholar can drum better than I and I've got to learn under him now, I'll quit." And he did. He quit drumming entirely and started playing clarinet from that time on. I never heard him play clarinet but I understand he played it until he was killed when hit by a car sometime later.

Of course Streckfus liked my drumming or he wouldn't have hired me. He liked the whole band. He used to use a white band out of Davenport, Iowa every year. They were jazz bands, too, or supposed to be. They called them jazz bands. But I guess he was losing money with the white bands. Red Nichols played on the boat one time, and also Miff Mole. Some of the white musicians didn't like the idea of playing with Fate, even though he was as light as any of them. I think that's why Mr. Streckfus wanted all Negroes.

The first year we went up the river we didn't do good at all. It was pitiful. We played up the Missouri River and I think people used to come on the boat more for curiosity than anything else. And they sat down and looked at us. They'd advertise before we got there that we were colored. So people wouldn't be disappointed. Fate Marable and his Jaz-E-Saz band, with Louis Armstrong, Baby Dodds, and so forth down the line. It was embarrassing to have the people stare at us but I didn't care about that. I looked at it this way: "Well, I'm doing something big or else there wouldn't be such astonishment." Often when we went to a town nobody would dance. Then when we'd go back for a second trip that same day, the boat would be packed.

Hannibal, Missouri was a hard place. We played one trip out of there, and had an excursion for the women and children in the daytime. We had a nice load, not full capacity but a nice load. At night we had only a few, and what was there just sat down and looked at us. And do you think they started dancing? No. They just sat and stared. That was from nine o'clock until eleven o'clock. Nobody danced. We'd take an intermission, go off, come back, and they'd still look at us. And then later on the mayor or somebody ordered another trip back there. He ordered a special chartered trip. My God, you couldn't get them off the boat; the boat was packed to capacity. I think the first time it was a surprise for the people. They had never before seen Negroes on the boat. They saw Negro roustabouts but had never seen a Negro with a tie and collar on, and a white shirt, playing music. They just didn't know what to make of it. But they really liked it. They were the dancingest people I ever found on the boat.

Sometimes the people would stand on the wharf and listen to the music. The boat was tied to the wharf and we'd play there for about a half hour before we'd ship out. That was partly to attract people. We also had dancing on the boat while it was docked. Lots of people would feel more secure when it was standing than when it was running. And the people on the boat were not the rowdy kind. We were lucky to have just nice people. If they weren't nice before they got on the boat, they were gentlemen and ladies while on it. They had some pretty tough guys around like bouncers to keep order. No liquor was served and there was no gambling, excepting raffles for candy.

The band played strictly for dancing. We played all the standards of the day and we used to make the classics into dance tunes. There was a sign up "Requests filled" and the people could ask for special numbers. We played eleven or twelve numbers, and every one of them had an encore to it. Then we had only a fifteen minute intermission, and started all over again. We worked pretty hard with that band.

But we didn't play many blues on the boat. The white people didn't go for blues like they do now. They try them now but they don't know the blues. They think any slow number is a blues type. That's wrong. Blues is blues. In New Orleans we used to play the blues and the very lowest type of dancers used to love such things. They were played very slow and fellows and their girl friends would stand almost still and just make movements. It was rowdy music, and yet it wasn't rowdy in a way, either. They often expressed some tragedy, just like *Frankie and Johnny. Frankie and Johnny* was one of this style of blues they used to sing a long time ago. It was about some woman and her man. Another one was *Ace in the Hole.* Those are really sporting numbers, which were played in the sporting houses, or when sporting people would get together.

The blues are something like a man drinking. If he drinks to extreme it's because there's something on his mind. And it's so deeply on his mind that the only cure he thinks he can find is a bottle. The blues is something of that sort. It may come from trouble in one's home, with his people, his wife or something, domestic troubles perhaps. That's what blues are. Something like this song, *Laugh, Clown, Laugh*. Regardless of how heavy your heart may be you can't give in to that and make the people know you're sorry. You've got to make them laugh. That's the same with the blues.

In New Orleans we played the blues in very slow tempo. Blues today aren't played as slow as in the old days. It used to be so draggy. I've heard white people say at a dance, "We don't want any of that dead march music. That sounds like a funeral march." Well, they didn't know any different. The colored people understood. The only way the colored people could express themselves was through blues, that perhaps nobody understood but themselves. That's the way they expressed themselves to themselves. It's very unnatural for some people, especially white people. In a way a white man has always had his chance to do anything that he wanted to. A Negro's chances are always limited.

The Negro had something to be blue for. He could go only so far and then he was cut out, regardless of how good he was. Quite naturally, when he thinks about it, that he's in a limited place in life, why he gets blue about it. Then he sits down, and he'll either whistle to himself, or pat his foot, or do something. And maybe he sings some song that's very slow, and he takes his time to express himself in his way. When another guy comes along, he hears the tune and says "What is this guy doing?" and asks, "What's the name of that tune?" The fellow answers, "Oh, just blues." And the second guy might ask, "Why blue?" and he answers, "Well, I got the blues, that's all it is." It's getting rid of your feelings within yourself. And it is expressed with a song. And it must have the feeling with it. If an individual doesn't have the feeling with the blues it doesn't mean anything.

I've heard some wonderful blues singers. I've listened to Ma Rainey sing the blues time and time again. And she would sing blues with words that coped with the situation. Like Mamie Smith. She had a voice and sang words that made you feel very sad. Bessie Smith was the same way. I think Bessie had one of the silver tones of blues singers. That's my opinion. Mamie Smith's voice was a little higher than alto, and Bessie Smith had a real clear alto voice. Ma Rainey had a baritone voice. Between the three singers, for my part, I would rather hear Bessie.

I didn't hear blues singers in St. Louis but I heard practically all the bands that were around there at the time we were on the riverboats. I used to like St. Louis very much. Dewey Jackson had a band there and so did Charlie Creath. And there was a place called Jazzland where they had a band. It was a rendezvous for most of the colored traveling acts that came from other places like Chicago. Sometimes, but very seldom, we would sit in with the St. Louis bands. Everybody that was working on the boat was known there and Louis and I used to travel together most of the time. And when we'd sit in there, we'd break it up. Naturally, I knew how to work with Louis and Louis knew how to work with me, so it turned out very nice. I met this drummer Red Muse, who was supposed to be very sensational, in St. Louis. It was a place called the Chauffeur's Club, a night club joined to a hotel. I was with Fate Marable and everybody was hollering when we came in the place. His drumming was very sensational, very good. He'd throw sticks and things like that. I was actually afraid to sit down there. But one night Fate played piano, and Louis played trumpet and I played drums, and we broke up the place. So I had no more bother with Muse after that. Before that I was scared to death. But I shimmied when I drummed and that took the eyes of the people. It was something different and made a very good impression.

My drumming improved a great deal on the boats but eventually Louis and I left because of a misunderstanding which we had with the bosses. Streckfus wanted us to play differently and he told Marable so. Well, Fate Marable had been with Streckfus so long that anything Streckfus asked for he'd tell us to do, even if it meant breaking our necks. The Streckfuses were musicians and they knew what they wanted and they wanted us to beat a different time than we had been using. Some of the older people on the boat couldn't dance to our music and Streckfus wanted to introduce what he called toddle time. It was really two-four time but he wanted four beats to the measure. It's what they are doing today. To me, four beats was all wrong. It has a tendency to speed up the music. But for the older people it was easier since instead of dancing to a step, they would just bounce around. Louis was also to play differently from what he had been used to. And I just couldn't do this toddle time on my drums. I felt that it would change me so much from my way of drumming, and from what I had learned and had been doing all those many years.

Louis couldn't do what they wanted him to do either. Well, we were the stars on the boat and we felt that if we were the stars, why monkey with us. We had already made a reputation with our music and the people were satisfied. So finally Louis and I left the boat together after handing in written resignations. That was about the first of September, 1921.

I often think what a shame it was that our riverboat band never recorded.[2] If they had, people would really have heard something pretty. It was just like a clock. Even if we got off one or two beats, somebody knew it and told us about it. It made me very sad to leave the Marable outfit. I had been attached to the band for three years and that was a long time to be with a special bunch of people. But I soon joined another group in which I was just as happy—the King Oliver Band.

[2] Although the Marable band with Baby and Louis never recorded, it did make a movie while Baby was a member. In 1919 the band made a short while playing on the top deck. Baby recalled seeing the movie, but said of it: "I don't remember where and don't remember how they did look. I suppose all right, but there weren't any sound effects. You'd just see me in the motions."

III
The Oliver Band

"We worked to make music, and we played music to make people like it."

I HAD just quit the river boat and was in New Orleans when Joe Oliver wanted me. Although Oliver had been in the Ory band when the members walked off the stand and left me alone playing drums, he thought about sending for me when his own drummer, Minor Hall, left the outfit. Oliver was playing in San Francisco at the time and my brother John played clarinet for him. When he learned of Joe's intention John said, "No, that guy can't play enough drums. He never will play. He drinks too much." But Davey Jones, who had played with me on the riverboats, was also in the Oliver band, although he had switched from mellophone to saxophone. Jones told Oliver, "If you can get that fellow, you'd better get him. Don't let him get away from you or some day you'll be sorry. That fellow is just as big a drawing card as Louis Armstrong." So Joe decided to send for me.

When I got there the first piece of music they put in front of me was *Canadian Capers*. I asked Joe how he was going to play it. He said from the left hand corner to the right hand corner; from top to bottom. The trio was in the middle of the number. I said "Kick off," and Joe kicked off. I read that piece of music down, from side to side and went back to the trio. I had played that number once and knew it, so I began playing my own style of drums. It was a jitney dance hall where everybody paid to get in the ring and dance, but people began leaving the ring to come over to the bandstand. Some even asked who I was and where I came from. Quite naturally it made Joe Oliver feel very happy to see people leave the dance floor and stop to listen to me. Davey Jones said to Joe, "I told you so." My brother was dumbfounded. He later told me, "You surprised me. How did you learn to drum like that?" I answered him, "That was my inspiration: to show you someday that I could drum. And I did."

We played for dancing at the Pergola dance hall in Frisco. The band then included Joe, who played cornet, my brother John on clarinet, Davey Jones who played alto sax, Honoré Dutrey on trombone, Lil Hardin on piano, Jimmie Palao, who played violin, and Eddie Garland, on bass fiddle. The band included a violin because we also played some theatre dates.

In Frisco we had some trouble and the local union hated to take us in. We were booked at the California Theatre as King Oliver's Creole Band. When the band went on for a matinee some little smart guy in the audience said, "I thought you said those guys were Creoles. Those guys are no Creoles. Those are niggers!" Of the whole band only Joe Oliver and Dutrey could talk Creole fluently, so they began to speak it very fast. The people just stared and that ended that episode, but afterwards the theater was no good. Meanwhile the Pergola dance date, which was supposed to be a long booking, had also fallen through, and with it my marriage fell through.

I had been married in 1912 to a girl named Odell Johnson. We had got acquainted through her two brothers, one of whom used to like to drink with me. She also liked music and I was married to her from 1912 until 1921. She stayed in New Orleans when I left for the West Coast and after two weeks I was to send for her. Of course when the job closed down I could not send for her. When I wrote for some personal papers she answered by saying that if I had lost part of my tail out there I could stay, as far as she was concerned. So after nine years together we separated at that time.

The Oliver band stayed out on the coast about fifteen months. After the dance hall on Market Street closed down I went with Ory and Mutt Carey. We played dances around Fresno, San Jose and Santa Cruz. Eddie Garland and I also played with the Oliver band whenever the dates didn't conflict. But we didn't call him Eddie Garland; we called him Montudie. Ory also had a good band at that time which included Ory on trombone, Wade Whaley on clarinet, and Mutt Carey on cornet. We played much the same sort of thing that Ory plays today: *Tiger Rag, Maple Leaf Rag, High Society,* and some blues.

Then Lil Hardin left the Oliver band and came back to Chicago.

The Oliver Band

Then Dutrey left the band and came back to Chicago. That left only King Oliver, my brother and myself, of the group that later played together in Chicago. That's when we picked up Bertha Gonsoulin. Bertha was a very nice woman, very quiet. She had classical training, too. We started a dance hall in Oakland and did very well. We had Bertha at the door and Mutt Carey's wife played piano. We had a nice business in Oakland. I think it was only Friday and Sunday that we played. Ory was in that outfit, since Dutrey was gone. Otherwise it was the same outfit: John, Joe, Eddie Garland and myself.

In 1922 King Oliver took his band to Chicago where we played in the Lincoln Gardens. Eddie Garland, Jimmie Palao and Davey Jones stayed on in California but I went east with the rest of the Oliver band. That's where Louis joined the band. He and I had worked together on the boat, and we quit together. After he got to Chicago Joe Oliver said he'd send for Louis. Everybody wondered whether he'd let Louis play first or second. And Joe said, "It's my band. What am I going to do, play second?" So Louis joined the band in Chicago in 1923, and played second cornet under Joe. The dance hall where we played was first called the Royal Gardens but it was later changed to Lincoln Gardens. I don't remember whether it was the Royal Gardens when I first went there or whether the name had already been changed. It was merely a hall with benches placed around for people to sit on. There was a balcony with tables on one side and the whole interior was painted with lively, bright colors. I would judge that the Gardens held about six or seven hundred people and many a night I've seen it filled up. When it was very full there would be a lot of people on the floor but dancing was nearly impossible because they used to bump into each other, and, of course, that's not dancing. But the people came to dance. One couldn't help but dance to that band. The music was so wonderful that they had to do something, even if there was only room to bounce around.

It was a dance band that liked to play anything. We didn't choose any one number to play well. We had the sort of band that, when we played a number, we all put our hearts in it. Of course that's why we could play so well. And it wasn't work for us, in those days, to play. Nobody took the job as work. We took it as play, and we loved it. I used to hate when it was time to knock off. I would drum all night till about three o'clock, and when I went home I would dream all night of drumming. That showed I had my heart in it, and the others had the same heart that I had. We worked to make music, and we played music to make people like it. The Oliver band played for the comfort of the people. Not so they couldn't hear, or so they had to put their fingers in their ears, nothing like that. Sometimes the band played so softly you could hardly hear it, but still you knew the music was going. We played so soft that you could often hear the people's feet dancing. The music was so soothing and then when we put a little jump into it the patrons just had to dance!

In those days I used to love to drum all the numbers. But I especially enjoyed the way we played *Someday Sweetheart*. It's a number so many guys think they know but they don't play it right. It is made up of triplets and it was really beautiful. My brother John came in with the melody in the lower register, slow and nice and easy, and the band backed him up with slow triplets. Other wonderful numbers were *Riverside Blues* and *Snake Rag*. Louis had a number called *Gully Low* and Lil's composition was *Pencil Papa*. We were all so ambitious. Somebody would suggest a number, and we would play it and experiment with different keys to see which would sound the best. Working with the Oliver band was a beautiful experience.

Dippermouth Blues was a number that the whole band worked out. Each member of the outfit contributed his own part. It was named for Louis, whom we called Dipperbill and Blathermouth, but everybody had his part in composing the thing. When the number didn't have a drum part I said I would make one and I put that part of *Dippermouth* in. The drummers have used it ever since. They don't do it right but they do it well enough to get by with it. But the really fine thing about the number was the way we worked it out together. There was no one individual star, but everybody had to come through. It made us feel so good to know that we had done our part towards helping everybody in the outfit. And when we worked a number out and rehearsed it we always played it that way. The only time *Dippermouth* was changed was when Louis went with Fletcher Henderson and they called the number *Sugarfoot Stomp*. But it was *Dippermouth* just the same.

The Oliver Band was traditional and Joe was always doing things according to the New Orleans tradition. Sometimes when the band started a number there would be one beat on the bass drum, or the

The Oliver Band

piano would have a couple of notes to pick up, or even Joe on the cornet. But it wasn't more than a couple of notes. It is New Orleans tradition that when there is an introduction everybody hits that introduction. The whole band had to start together and finish together. No sloppy start or ending was permitted. We did these things correctly and that is why our band sounded so good.

Even the lineup on the bandstand was in New Orleans tradition. From our left to right there was the bass, then the piano, then the clarinet, next to the clarinet was Louis on second trumpet and Joe was next to him. Next to Joe was Dutrey on trombone, and my drums were next to the trombone. The banjo was next to the piano but either a little in back or in front of the piano, next to the treble keys. The lineup at the Lincoln Gardens bandstand was arranged in such a way as to make the music sound better. In other words, it gave good balance and improved the sound.

Every number sounded very good and the band had a very large repertoire. We could play a four or five-hour dance without repeating a number. Of course people usually asked for repeats on some numbers and we often had to play encores, so we didn't actually use our whole repertoire in the course of one night's work. And after we started recording we didn't have as many numbers as before because we would go over the numbers that we had recorded. This made us very familiar with them but it was not monotonous because it all sounded so beautiful.

Not all the people came to the Lincoln Gardens to dance. Some of the white musicians came to hear our band. Benny Goodman, Jess Stacy, Frank Teschemacher, Dave Tough, Bud Freeman and Ben Pollack used to come to listen. George Wettling came when he was still in knee pants. Other musicians listened but they never sat in with the Oliver band for the simple reason that it was an untouchable band. The band had everything so perfect that it was recognized as tops. We were getting fifty-five dollars a week at the time, and there were a lot of bands around that weren't getting half that. The other musicians didn't ask for tips on playing jazz music because they thought we were the type of people who wouldn't say anything or explain things. They were wrong. Everybody in the outfit would talk, but in those days they were afraid to talk with us about the music.

One of the most frequent visitors at the Gardens was Paul Whiteman. His band was playing at the Granada at Cottage Grove and Sixty-seventh. They got off before we did and every night the whole band would come rushing in there like mad. They had tuxedos on and on the cuffs of their sleeves they'd jot down different notes we played. Joe Oliver did one peculiar thing which kept a lot of them guessing. He would cut the titles off the numbers, so no one could come up and look at the number to get it for his own outfit. Sometimes they asked Joe what a certain number was called and he would say anything that came into his mind. That's how some of the numbers got different names. Fellows working in other bands would give the numbers the names which Joe gave them, and it was all wrong.

But they all admired King Oliver's style of playing. It was wonderful. You won't get another King Oliver. He very seldom played open horn. He played mostly muted. He'd put his hand over the mouth of the trumpet and it would sound like a mouth organ. We used to call him "Harmonica." That's where the wah-wah mutes came from but the others didn't know how to use them. Of course Louis Armstrong, who played second cornet in the band, used an open horn. Louis was so versatile that Joe would blow just a couple of notes while we were playing and tell Louis where the breaks would come, and they worked them right in the number. They were the only two that worked together in that way. John and Dutrey used to come along with the counterpoint or harmony to correspond. But otherwise Joe and Louis worked those things out alone.

Joe was always making suggestions for the improvement of the band. In 1923 I used very heavy sticks. One day Joe told me, "I want to try to get you to beat light," and he brought me some wire brushes. It was a new thing and I was probably the first guy that ever worked with wire brushes in this part of the country. But I still beat heavy even with the brushes and Joe said, "You'd beat heavy with two wet mops. Give me those things. Take your sticks back." I didn't like the brushes and couldn't get anything out of them. It seemed lazy to me. But I realized that I should learn to beat lighter with the sticks. I worked on this and began getting very technical with the drum sticks. That is why I can beat so light now with sticks. Joe Oliver was the cause of that. In those days, if you didn't do what the fellows told you to do, they were through with you. You had to do those things which would improve the outfit and the sound of the band, and that was that.

The Oliver Band

Oliver's band was the sort of group where you could use your own experiences and eventually get a chance to work them out with the outfit. I used woodblocks on my part in *Dippermouth,* but on most numbers I used the shells or rims of the drums instead. I did very little on the wood blocks, and much more on the shells. They weren't as sharp. The wood block gave a tone that was too shrill and sharp for the band. The sound of the rim was much better. It was up to me to bring out the different expressions for the outfit. If I would be drumming straight and felt that a roll would bring out an expression I used that. Or if I were playing along and felt that beating the cymbal would help the number, I would do that. It was up to all of us to improve the band in its jazz, and I had to do my part.

It was my job to study each musician and give a different background for each instrument. When a man is playing it's up to the drummer to give him something to make him feel the music and make him work. That's the drummer's job. Those words were told to me by my teacher, Brundy, when I first started to drum. The drummer should give the music expression, shading, and the right accompaniment. It's not just to beat and make a noise. I played differently for each instrument in the band. With the piano I tried to play as soft as I could with a low press roll; not to soft, of course, but just the right volume. I didn't use brushes because they did not give shading to the drum tone. For my brother I would play the light cymbal on the top. And for Dutrey I would hit the cymbal the flat way, so it would ring, but not too loud. For Joe and Louis I would hit the cymbal a little harder and make it ring more.

I studied each player individually. I had to study their method of improvising and to know what they intended to do. And when the band came in as a whole, in ensemble, I had to do something different again. But at all times I heard every instrument distinctly. I knew when any of them were out of tune or playing the wrong note. I made that a distinct study. Those of us who worked with the King Oliver Band had known each other so long we felt that we were almost related. That outfit had more harmony and feeling of brotherly love than any I ever worked with. And playing music is just like having a home. If you don't have harmony with each other you don't get along. If you've got a family of ten, regardless of what goes on, if you haven't got harmony you know it's a terrible house. I feel the same thing applies to musicians. If you haven't got harmony in your band, you haven't got a good band. And everybody should do his part to the best of his ability. I've been in many an outfit where there was no harmony. In such groups a smile goes a long way. Because when you are happy and someone is glum you'll come pretty near washing that glumness out. But if a group lacks harmony, laughter and heart-gladness, you haven't got a good group.

We did a lot of kidding around in the Oliver band. Of course, Louis was the comical man in the band. My brother was serious but he had play days too. He didn't pull tricks but he often made a remark to kid the others. When he wanted to get one on me he'd say, "Oh my God, I'll bet you he's drunk!" Well, that was a big thing with me since Bill Johnson and I were the only ones in the Oliver group that drank. Sometimes we used to play around on the bandstand. Joe had only one good eye and one day we were throwing spitballs. John threw one at me, and Dutrey threw one at Louis, and Louis threw one at John. Some of the spitballs passed Joe so close that he could hear the whizz as they went by. Joe said, "Listen, if some of you guys hit me in my good eye, I'm going to shoot you." One night we laughed at him and he said, "You don't believe I've got a gun, huh? You don't think I'm going to shoot you." And he opened his cornet case, and there he had a gun. Well, then things quieted down. He wasn't going to shoot anybody, but that was his way of stopping the spitball business.

Joe may have carried that gun because he was afraid of holdups, too. I do know he used to carry quite a sum of money all the time and it may have been that. I've seen the time that Joe would have four or five hundred dollars in his pocket. Only the band fellows knew that, though. There were some tough guys around 31st Street so I can see why he was afraid. But naturally we thought he was carrying the gun for us.

We were bad, not really bad, but mischievous. And we'd have a lot of fun playing music. And you can't play music anyway with a grouch. You'd better leave the grouch at home. The important part about playing music is the idea of having a happy heart and a happy mind. We had it then. People would see us, the band as a whole, laughing and joking and playing. Joe was also a great kidder. He would kid you so it would make your heart ache, but you had to

The Oliver Band

laugh. He always carried the group with him and it was impossible to sit up there with a grouch.

Sometimes Louis and I used to have some special fun while playing. Louis would make something on his horn, in an afterbeat, or make it so fast that he figured I couldn't make it that fast, or he'd make it in syncopation or in Charleston time, or anything like that for a trick. And I would come back with something on the snare drums, and with an afterbeat on the bass drum, or a roll or something. But I had to keep the bass drum going straight because of the band. I couldn't throw the band. Louis and I would throw each other and pick it up ourselves and keep the band going. They would feel it, but no one in the audience knew anything about it. Usually this was only kidding, but it did happen when Louis and I were angry.

Once Louis and I had a regular scuffle at the Lincoln Gardens. We had been kidding and joking and when I said something the whole band would sway with me. Then Louis would say something else and the whole bunch swayed with him. One word led to another. We were kidding during the intermission period, and it got pretty hot. Then we got up to each other and clinched and scratched each other and I tore his silk shirt. We all used to wear those silk shirts then, white Japanese silk shirts. By then the whole band was interested. Some said, "I got my money on Satchmo," and another, "I got my money on Babe." It was stopped because we had to play music but our silk shirts were very ragged by then. We had to finish the night's work with those torn shirts on and everybody wanted to know what had happened. I had to tell the story about eight or nine times, the night around. But the people never knew the difference. After the little humbug that Louis and I had, we played just the same. They wouldn't know. That is one thing we had that I don't think the white musicians have. We played music and laughed and joked all the time with it, until it looked so much like fun.

But we worked very hard. I doubt if there was one person in that outfit that had a dry shirt when we got done. So that meant everybody worked pretty hard. But of course you can't play music and be angry. Because when playing music you must have a clear heart and clear mind. If you don't you can't give your best. In some groups there are misunderstandings and some hold malice and show it. But in the outfit that we had, this King Oliver outfit, regardless of what happened, or how angry someone was, you would never know the difference. That's the big thing about music. You can't be mad or hold a grudge and play good music. If you've got a grudge against somebody you must put it down till you've finished playing music.

In the Oliver band everybody had a good time, including the master of ceremonies, King Jones, who did the announcing at the Gardens. If anything special came along he would tell about it, and he had his own way of acting. He used to dance in front of the band and he got such a kick out of it himself that the patrons also enjoyed it. Sometimes he pretended to lead the band. Of course he didn't know anything about the music and it never interfered with our work. The people got a big kick out of it because they knew he didn't know what he was doing and they thought we were going along with him. But we just played our own style and paid no attention to him.

There was lots of fun in the Gardens but sometimes things got pretty rough, too. Sunday matinees were the only occasions when youngsters could get in the place, and they had many fights. Of course, it was our job to keep on playing. Even if you're on a ship and it's sinking, you've still got to play. That's one thing I don't like about music. You can't go any place, you've got to stay there and play. One Sunday some of the youngsters started a pistol fight on the balcony of the Gardens. We were playing when the shooting started and when the guy shot twice, Joe got up and ran. Louis got up and ran, my brother ran behind the piano and Dutrey also made haste to get away. But I just sat in my chair and played my drums. When it was over they put the guys out and carried them to jail. The others in the band thought I was a fool to stay at my drums and when they asked me why I didn't run I answered, "Run for what? Where was I going to run? There was no need for me to run any place." I figured that if I ran I would be subject to a stray bullet and I might even run into it. They weren't shooting at me and I thought just sitting still was as safe as anything.

Nobody was killed and I guess it was a good thing that they couldn't serve liquor there or there might have been some killings. It was prohibition but I always had plenty to drink myself. Oliver didn't drink anything, Dutrey wasn't drinking anything, and neither was my brother nor Louis. But Bill Johnson and I drank plenty. Of course we never drank so much that it interfered with our playing. And none of the Oliver musicians used dope or marijuana. That's a recent trend that doesn't even go along with music, because it makes your reactions and your nerves go dead. It's worse than whiskey. Some of the white musicians wanted me to use it. I said "Oh, no. Get me some gin. I'll try that. Or some bourbon." In those days it was almost impossible to get whiskey for even eight dollars a pint. And when I first went with the Oliver band every girl in the place wanted to talk to me. It was pretty smooth but if a girl wouldn't buy me a pint of Old Taylor, she couldn't even talk to me. But if she bought me a pint of Old Taylor I would give her my undivided attention.

I had a lot of girl friends in those days but I also made some good friends among the band members. Dutrey was my best friend of all. He depended on me and he also felt sympathy for my drinking because in earlier days he, too, used to drink a lot. Dutrey stopped drinking because of his asthma which he contracted while in the navy during World War I. While he was on board ship he used to talk with a fellow who was on watch near the powder hold. The fellow on duty was a great talker and Dutrey would go inside the powder room and talk with him through the door so if the officers came around they wouldn't see anybody talking to the fellow on watch. One day when the fellow went off duty he forgot Dutrey was there and Dutrey went to sleep in the powder room. The next guy that came on duty closed the door. I don't remember how many hours he stayed in there, but when they took him out he was unconscious. It gave him asthma. His tongue was as black as any shoe and eventually his asthma killed him. He used an atomizer, though, and you would never know he had any trouble. He played trombone even though there was a lot of dust in the dance hall and the damp weather around Chicago was awfully hard on his throat.

Dutrey tried to make me save money. He knew how to economize, and when he went to buy something he usually would buy two if it was a good item of whatever it was. That's what he wanted me to do. And finally he broke me into the habit. He used to call me Tiger, because he claimed that when I got angry, I had such an awful way, just like a tiger.

He was a wonderful musician as well as a swell fellow. He played very sweet trombone. He wasn't a harsh man. He didn't play bop, bop, bop; nothing like that. He played everything pretty and it always corresponded in harmony with the others. He worked with the trumpet player, he didn't work by himself. And when he played it would blend with the trumpet. Al Wynn, who studied under Dutrey, plays in a similar style, although he's much rougher than Dutrey. Dutrey was always very smooth. Preston Jackson also played similarly, but he's also playing rougher now. If a trombonist played rough Dutrey wouldn't bother with him. If a person didn't come up to standard, the oldtimers of those days wouldn't have anything to do with him. And it made the youngsters feel so bad that they'd work twice as hard, and put out more effort. And it made better musicians of them.

Music was our main interest, but of course we had other interests too. Joe Oliver, for instance, was a great eater. Oh God, how he could eat! If he came to your home, you would have to make him a galvanized bucket full of lemonade. He had stopped drinking whiskey about 1918. I don't know if it was his health or not. Then he became a great lemonade drinker. And if you didn't have a dishpan full of biscuits for Joe you didn't have any biscuits. My brother was also a great bread eater. He could take a piece of meat about two inches around and eat up any loaf of bread. But John didn't eat so much otherwise. Joe Oliver, however, was just a big eater. If you would invite him to your house you'd better have a couple of chickens because he would eat two of them.

Many of the fellows in the Oliver band were also great sports fans. They were all baseball fans. My brother knew every baseball player from Ty Cobb's days. He and Oliver also used to shoot pool, and so did Dutrey. Dutrey and John used to like to play whist. I never liked pool or cards and I imagine my life has been duller on account of that. The others liked sports of all kinds, especially racing and boxing. John got so emotional at boxing matches that sometimes if you sat beside him he would punch you on the nose.

But most of our life revolved around our music. When we played in the Lincoln Gardens at night we also had an evening job at a Quincy Street restaurant operated by Husk O'Hare. There we played dinner music. We played our regular band numbers, only mixed in with a few waltzes and some pop tunes of the day. It was very inconvenient for me because I had to move my entire drum set on the street car. When the street car came along I'd have to hand the drums into it, first my snare drums and then the bass drum. Quite naturally

Baby Dodds (third from left) at Mente's bag factory, 1912. *Courtesy John Dodds*

Baby Dodds (far left) with Fate Marable's band on the SS *Sidney*, 1918. To the right of Baby are Bebé Ridgley, Joe Howard, Louis Armstrong, Fate Marable, David Jones, Johnny Dodds, Johnny St. Cyr, and George "Pops" Foster. *From the Al Rose Collection, Hogan Jazz Archive, Tulane University*

Close-up of Baby Dodds (far left) with Fate Marable's band, *ca.* 1920, aboard the SS *Sidney* at St. Louis. To the right of Baby are Joe Howard, Pops Foster, Johnny St. Cyr, David Jones, and Sam Dutrey. On the front row are Grant Cooper, Fate Marable, and Louis Armstrong. *Courtesy John Dodds*

Baby Dodds's best friend in King Oliver's Creole Jazz Band, the trombonist Honoré Dutrey. *Courtesy State Historical Society of Wisconsin*

Baby Dodds and his first automobile, *ca.* 1923. *Courtesy John Dodds and the State Historical Society of Wisconsin*

Baby Dodds and his drums. *Courtesy State Historical Society of Wisconsin*

King Oliver's Creole Jazz Band, Chicago, 1923. Clockwise from left: Honoré Dutrey, Baby Dodds, Joseph "King" Oliver, Bill Johnson, Johnny Dodds, Lil Hardin, and Louis Armstrong. *From the Al Rose Collection, Hogan Jazz Archive, Tulane University*

Mrs. Tommy Ladnier, Tommy Ladnier, and Baby's wife, Irene, sitting on the runningboard of Baby's $1470.40 Oldsmobile, *ca.* 1923. *Courtesy John Dodds*

Baby Dodds's favorite picture of himself, 1923. *Courtesy John Dodds and the State Historical Society of Wisconsin*

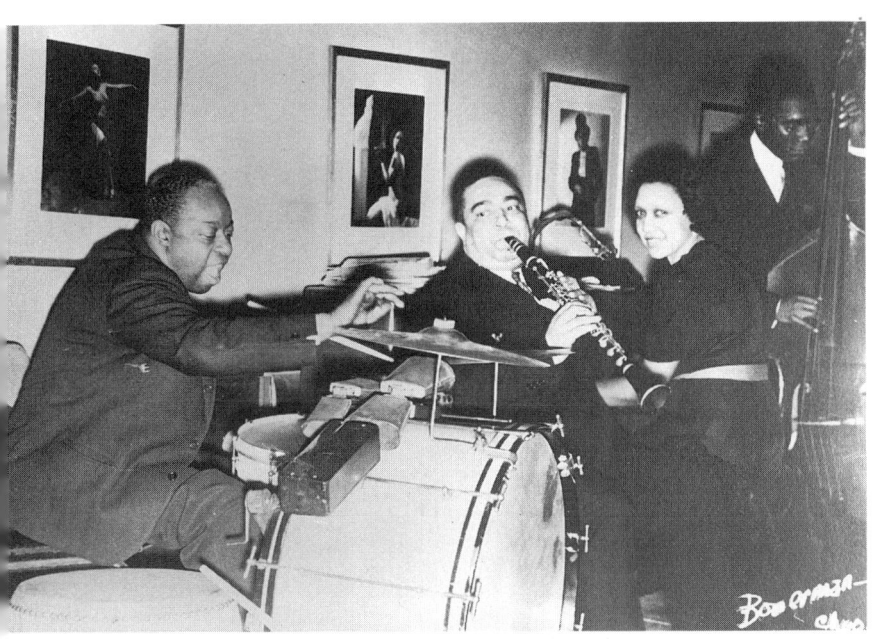

Baby Dodds performing with Jimmie Noone, Mada Roy, and Bill Anderson, 1942. *Courtesy State Historical Society of Wisconsin*

Baby Dodds recording with Bunk Johnson's band, 1944. *Courtesy Frances Reitmeyer*

Baby Dodds playing the snare drum. *Courtesy State Historical Society of Wisconsin*

Bunk Johnson's band in New York, 1945. Back row: Jim Robinson, Bunk Johnson, Alcide "Slow Drag" Pavageau, Lawrence Marrero. Front row: Baby Dodds, Alton Purnell, George Lewis. *Courtesy Bill Russell*

Baby Dodds, Pops Foster, an unidentified friend, and Jimmy Archey in France, 1948. *Courtesy John Dodds and the State Historical Society of Wisconsin*

Baby Dodds performing with Miff Mole's band at the Beehive in Chicago, 1948. From the left: Darnell Howard, Art Gronwall, Freddie Greenleaf, Miff Mole, and Baby. *Courtesy Frances Reitmeyer*

Baby Dodds at the Stuyvesant Casino, New York, *ca.* 1949. *Courtesy Duncan P. Schiedt*

Natty Dominique and Baby Dodds, 1954. *Courtesy John Dodds and Bill Russell*

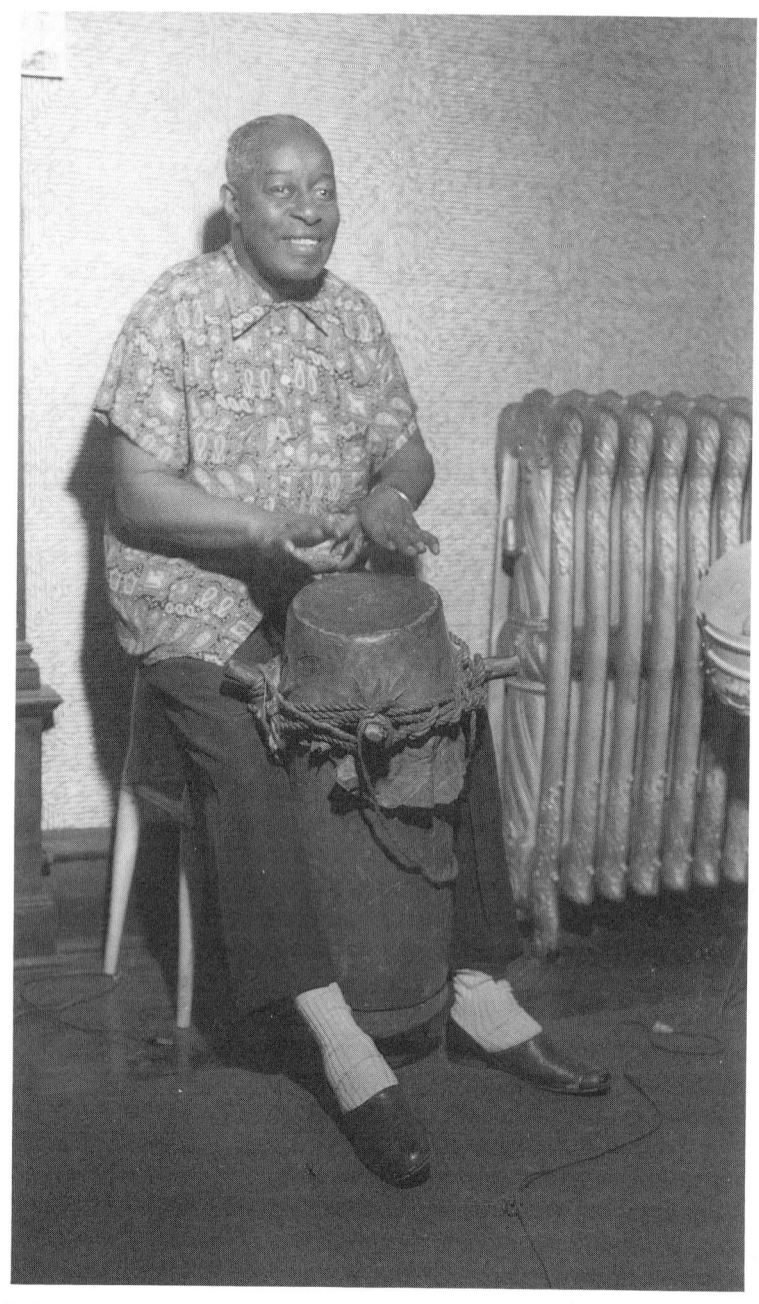

Baby Dodds "fooling around with a tom tom" in his home, 1954. *Courtesy Bill Russell*

someone always saw me with that load and would help me in with the drums. It was pretty bad, especially on those cold wintry days. I never dropped anything, though, and never had the misfortune of having any broken drum head of any sort.

It was because of having to move my drums all the way across Chicago on a street car that I bought my first automobile. And I paid cash for it, too. No one wanted to co-sign for me. The band men knew I drank all the time and they were afraid to co-sign for fear they would be responsible for my death. That was around 1923. I asked King Oliver to sign with me and he said no. So did Dutrey and Miss Major, the woman whom I worked for at the Gardens. Finally I asked my brother, John. He said "No, indeed. I'll never sign for you to have an automobile. You don't keep whiskey out of you long enough." Well, that was all right with me. I didn't want to use the cash I had saved up but I went down to the bottom of my trunk and dug out the money. I bought the car with cash. It was an Oldsmobile and cost me $1470.40, cash on the line.

I bought the car at 63rd Street and the man drove it down to the Gardens. I had never driven a car myself except one which I drove about fifteen feet into a barn when I was about nine years old. This car was painted bright red, like a fire wagon. Well, when we came out from working we all came out together. I hadn't said a thing to any of the others. I wanted it to be a surprise since they had all turned me down on the co-signing. I went up to the car and kicked the tires. I opened the doors and looked inside. Everybody noticed what I was doing and John shouted, "Hey what are you doing with that man's car? You'll get in trouble." I answered, "I'm not afraid." Then King Oliver said to me, "Is that your car?" I said, "What do you think?" Of course, Joe started to laugh and Louis, who knew it was mine, also laughed. Finally he admitted, "That's Babe's car." When I told them that I bought it with cash they really were surprised.

Then I asked, "Who's going to ride with me?" Joe Oliver said, "You'll never kill me." My brother said, "No, indeed. I've got three children." Even Dutrey said, "Well, Tiger, I'm sorry. I'm going to turn you down." Louis came out and said, "Oh, you're not going to get me in that, Pops." Finally Lil Hardin came out. She and I had been very good friends, even in San Francisco, and I said, "Well, Lil, you'll ride with me." She answered, "Sure, I'll ride with you." She wasn't a bit afraid although all the others were. I knew that she could drive a car and I admitted that I needed her help anyway. So she got in with me and we passed the rest of the guys on the street and I honked the horn at them. After that, Dutrey, who lived in the same house with me, used to ride to work in my car. All the others wanted to know, "How does he drive?" Dutrey said I did all right. But John commented, "If that guy doesn't stay off liquor, he's going to kill himself." Dutrey said, "I don't think so. Baby doesn't drink and drive."

After that Louis and Lil used to ride in my Oldsmobile. He was sweet on Lil but I didn't know it. Lil used to ride in front with me and Louis in the back and Louis would lean over the back seat and talk with Lil, and that's the way they got together in my car. After they were married I told them many times, "If it hadn't been for me you wouldn't be married."

In those days I got a new car nearly every year. It was easy from then on because a person who owns one car can always get another without a co-signer. But I'll bet I was in almost every jail around Chicago. The speed limit was twenty-five miles an hour but nobody drove a car twenty-five miles an hour. There weren't nearly as many cars on the street as today and I was always going thirty. When they raised the speed limit to thirty miles an hour I always went thirty-five. Every time I turned around I was in jail. But I didn't miss work because in those days the car could be put up to bail a person out of jail.

The longest I ever stayed in jail was twenty-four hours. I never got arrested without having to pay a fine. I had an accident down on Michigan Avenue near the Drake Hotel. They had just put the lights in and the amber showed up as I approached the corner. I had no intention of stopping but the guy in front of me stopped and I didn't. Of course I hit his car in the back. I had a very pretty 1924 Buick, and this white fellow had an old Ford. He and his wife were on their way to church, so oh my God, they yelled like they were half dead! Things got worse when they found out that my car was so beautiful and that we were having such a wonderful time. Well, it was white against black and it was pretty bad, that's all. They carried me to jail and I received the same treatment in jail as if I were a criminal and had killed somebody with a gun. They got everything on me they could. They charged me with assault and battery, reckless driving, speeding, and even with carrying a dangerous weapon. All this because I hit that fellow's car. I was scared to death. I got a lawyer but he didn't say very much. It cost me almost two hundred dollars to get out of that jam. And still I stayed in jail twenty-four hours and got a record for it. The accident was on a Sunday morning and they didn't hold court until Monday morning. There were a lot of show people in my car at the time and they all went in to court for me.

I knew a lot of people through my work with the Oliver band. It was when I was playing at the Lincoln Gardens that I met my second wife, Irene. It was on Christmas Eve of 1922. She had been at Lincoln Gardens listening to the band and dancing, and was going home when I caught up with her at the corner of Indiana and Thirty-first Street. I had a lot of little toys which I had purchased for John's children. I carried them to work because I did not want to go back home before going to John's place. Well, I had my arms full of toys, and I had been drinking, so naturally I dropped one of them. We were both waiting for the street car and Irene picked up the toy I dropped. I could hardly stand up and she sympathized with me and helped me on the street car. She carried some of the toys and thought it was a very nice thing for me to carry so many toys home for my brother's children.

The band members used to kid me a lot about Irene. They called us the old folks, and they couldn't figure out how such a quiet person as Irene would take up with such a wild fellow like me. Everybody tried to get a shine to her, but she wouldn't take to anybody but me. Shortly after we met on Christmas Eve we began going together and we got married in 1923. Her first husband had died but I wasn't divorced yet so we had to wait until that went through.

Irene has been wonderful about my work in music, having to be away from home a lot. She always understood. Of course when you're making a living for your family you have to do what the job calls for. Many homes have been broken on account of the traveling, but I figure those things would have broken anyway. Because if two people love each other they have confidence and they don't just jump up and run because of that. But it's a tough part of a musician's life. It was especially hard for John because of the children. Sometimes he'd come home so tired he didn't even see his children, and he'd have to get up the next night and go to work. But Irene and I always got along wonderfully.

Those were wonderfully happy days when I was with the Oliver

Band. It was a shame to see that band break up. But it had to bust up and I was one of the guys mainly responsible for breaking up the outfit. I was so high strung in those days. I was only a little thing, but very high strung. And that's one of the worst things about musicians. They all have tempers. I began to suspect that Oliver was cheating on us. When I first joined the band it was called "Our Band." After we commenced recording, and making so much money, Joe said it was his band. "This is my band," he said. Well, of course, that put a different feeling in the fellows. Next the royalties on the records we made for the Gennett company got smaller and smaller. Nobody saw the royalty checks but Oliver. They were in his name and had to be cashed by him. We had an argument when some of us wanted to see the checks. Joe Oliver wouldn't come up with the checks. In our minds that showed guilt although we didn't know for sure what the real story was. I talked with the others and by the time I got through talking they all felt like I did, and we decided to disband.

It was a sad thing. I felt awful blue about seeing that band break up. I would forget it one minute and the next minute it was right back in my mind again. It felt just like having a girl whom you like very much fall out with you. I felt as though I had lost something and a feeling of loneliness came over me. That's the way I felt when I left the Oliver outfit. It seemed as though something was missing from my life. It was pretty bad for a while.

King Oliver, of course, organized another band right away. He went on the road for a time and I think he played in New York. Then he returned to Chicago to play at the Plantation. He had a very good band. My brother was in it for a while and he had a fellow named Clifford Jones on drums. They called him "Snags" because he had some teeth missing. He was a very good drummer, a left-hand, trick drummer who threw his drum sticks in the air. It was very sensational because Joe had never had that type of drummer before. When he had me I was a straight drummer, although I had used my shimmy beat with the Oliver outfit occasionally.

I only played with King Oliver on one other occasion. It was around 1925 when Oliver was at the Plantation. Paul Barbarin, his drummer, took sick, and Oliver wanted to know if I would work in Paul's place. I had no regular job at the time but I knew that was

The Oliver Band

pretty stiff and didn't know whether I could do it or not. I told Joe I didn't think I could and he said, "Oh yes, you can. You can do anything." So I got up my courage and went over to play the floor show. That was tough to go in and play the show when I had not rehearsed it with the others. Nobody knew I was a strange drummer until the finale of the first show. There was a place that called for four measures of cowbells, and I missed these four measures. It changed the tempo and the girls who were dancing couldn't change the tempo in their routine. That's when they knew I was strange to the band. After that I had no more trouble though I only played in Paul's place for one night. Oliver had a big band of ten-twelve pieces at the time. He had Barney Bigard and Albert Nicholas on clarinets, Darnell Howard played violin, clarinet and sax, Ory on trombone, Bud Scott on guitar, and a fellow by the name of Bert Cobb on bass. Instead of Louis on second trumpet he had Bob Schoffner. He was a nice trumpet man, too. During the course of the evening we played some of the same numbers that we used to play with the smaller band in the Gardens. To me it didn't have the same meaning, but it sounded all right for a big band.

Years later, in 1935, Oliver came through Chicago again. He had a bunch of youngsters down south somewhere and he was planning a tour of Memphis and the lower South. He wasn't quite satisfied with the drummer and he wanted me with the outfit. I was never so surprised in my life. At the time I was playing with John's group at the New Plantation and I turned him down flat. He had a good sized outfit and I would have enjoyed working with him, and would have been happy to do all I could for the youngsters, and perhaps help Joe too. But I was playing with my brother and didn't think it would make sense to leave his outfit.

It really is a shame, though, that Oliver never got to Europe. That's where his band would really have been appreciated. In fact, the bands that are playing jazz in France today are trying to have the sort of band that King Oliver had in the early days. They use the same instrumentation, two trumpets, trombone, clarinet, bass viol, banjo, and drums. And it sounds very good, in my estimation. It certainly would have been a great thing, though, if King Oliver had gone to Europe before he died.

IV
Jazz in Chicago

"I think a drummer should be versatile. You can't go along with a one-track mind and be a good drummer."

SOON AFTER the Oliver band broke up my brother got a job down at Burt Kelly's Stables. Burt Kelly had been a banjo player and he used to play in the band there himself. But he really had brains and when he became boss he knew just how to run a place like that. As far as the band was concerned, he picked his men carefully. He knew exactly what he wanted. Since he was hiring a band just after the Oliver group split up he picked some of the men from that outfit to play at his place. From it he got my brother, Bill Johnson, and myself. Dutrey was also there, but just as a specialty for the first few nights. Kelly only wanted a small outfit, trumpet, clarinet, piano, drums and bass. Freddie Keppard played trumpet and Charlie Alexander, piano.

Burt Kelly's Stables was a regular night club, cabaret style, with singing waiters, and it was all on the second floor. They had harnesses and horse collars hanging around. It wasn't a very big place. The walls had been painted green, and then calcimined. People took knives and wrote on the wall, and the green came through. Some drew hearts and things like "Mamie and Jim," and sometimes they wrote dates on the wall. Often people used to walk all around the room and look at them to see if there was anything about someone they might know.

But I didn't last at Kelly's Stables very long. I was there much less than a year when my brother had to get rid of me. Burt Kelly said my drumming was pretty bad. In fact, he thought I was the rottenest drummer he had ever heard. Some of the other members of the outfit also left. One night Freddie Keppard came in pretty drunk, and he got fired. That was about 1925 and that was when my brother got Natty Dominique to play trumpet. Dominique stayed with John until the place closed down. Bill Johnson also left Kelly's Stables. He was drinking one night, and fell off the bandstand. He was about six foot two and it was quite a fall. He was laid up for a long while after that and never returned to John's outfit.

I went back to Kelly's Stables in 1928. John's drummer, Frank Bates, opened up his own poolroom and he tried to run the poolroom and also work his job at Burt Kelly's. It proved too much of a job for him. He would stay awake in his poolroom where he was making money, and when he got to his job at Burt Kelly's he would go to sleep. It didn't work and John had to let him go. Then John got me back in the outfit. I left the Charlie Elgar band to go with him. Of course he had been there since we first started there in 1924. And Kelly was glad to hear my drumming. I was wide awake, and coming after this fellow Frank Bates, who was always tired and sleepy, it made the outfit sound much better. Kelly commented to John how wonderful my drumming sounded and he could hardly believe it when John told him, "Well, that's the same guy I had before; that's my brother." In fact Kelly was so pleased that he had a light put on the post right by the drums. He said, "We've got to see the guy that's doing so much drumming."

At Kelly's Stables we only played for dancing and for the waiters to sing. We played mostly pop stuff, but we put a little jazz twist to it. We never played anything straight, but even oldtime numbers like *Dardanella* we played in our own inimitable way. We would jazz the numbers and play them in different tempos. We always tried to find the tempo that would fit the number and make it sound very soothing, and still jumpy enough to put life in it. Because there were only white people there, we seldom played blues.

We used to have different nights for different groups of people who came in. There were special nights every week and sometimes groups would come in and have parties. We always knew in advance because they would call up and make reservations. Then we had a regular night for college people, I think it was Friday. Monday night was always theatrical night. Different theatrical groups from other cities would come in and they would be sure to have an outing at Kelly's Stables. It was a very nice custom. They would get acquainted with Chicago people and other show folks and it made it very nice for them.

We played at Kelly's Stables during prohibition days. They sold setups of ginger ale, ice and lemon, but no whiskey. Those who didn't bring their own whiskey were out of luck. But on New Year's Day of 1930 the government closed the place on what they called observation evidence. Although Kelly didn't sell any liquor they accused him of having liquor on the premises. And they closed it with my drums in the place. Finally my brother John got some official to go there and break the seal on the place and get my drums. I think that after they closed the Stables, Burt Kelly and his wife went to New Jersey and went into the real estate business.

For a while after the closing of Kelly's Stables we had no job, and then we went to a Chinese restaurant on Thirty-first Street. There was Freddie Keppard on trumpet, John on clarinet, a girl named Big Eye Lil on the piano, and me on drums. They had a show for people who were sitting around eating, and also dancing some of the time. We had a floor show with about eight girls in the line. In the whole show there were about eighteen people, and we only had four pieces in the band. For the dancing after the show I played practically the same way I had at Kelly's Stables. But for the show I chose a different style of drumming altogether.

Big Eye Lil played piano similar to the style of Lil Armstrong. Of course, we had played with Keppard years before, the first time we were in Kelly's Stables. Freddie Keppard had a style that most of the Creole fellows played in New Orleans. Of course it was his own style of jazz, but it was good. It was loud, too. He didn't use mutes, but played an open horn. He used to play on State and Thirty-fifth and you could hear him almost to Thirty-ninth and State. He was a big man, weighing about two hundred and fifty, and he actually could blow. It was both loud and pretty, and Keppard had an unusual and wonderful tone. However, he was a very fiery guy, and he would hit you over the head with his horn any time and think nothing about it. All those guys were high strung.

John was a very capable leader, though, and handled the men under him very well. He belonged to a club and various publishers brought new music to him when it first came out. I've seen him spend quite a bit of money to get books with various types of special music in them. When special groups came to the places where we played we were notified ahead of time and John would play the music they would like to hear. He had various college songs for college kids, and Sousa marches for army groups and for navy groups we would play songs like *Anchors Aweigh*. John was a very good reader and he would often play the violin parts on his clarinet. When we played I used to follow the different instruments and their parts, too. I had the same notes on my drum parts that the others had in their music books. And by following it I could tell if the others were playing right or wrong. If the others didn't play the same thing I had I knew they were wrong. And many a time I corrected some of the other members of that outfit. Lots of times I've picked Dominique for such things, because his trumpet part was practically the same as the part for my snare drum. I would bring him back and he always took such things very smoothly. He is one conscientious guy and always wanted to do everything as correctly as possible. And Dominique was very good at transposing. He'd copy the part and put it two notes lower for his trumpet. And John would often experiment with tempo. If he didn't like the tempo which we used for a number he would change it until he found one which suited him. Sometimes he tried sixteen different tempos before he got one which he thought fit a certain tune.

John was a pretty stiff fellow with his men. He tried to maintain good order at all times. He wanted all of us to show up for work in plenty of time. He and Dominique are the two most punctual people I have ever known. And when John said "play" he wanted you to be ready then, not a minute or two later. If he was angry he would not talk to the person who got him angry. And when he'd not talk to you you'd know there was dissatisfaction somewhere. But those things we'd sit down and talk over at intermission and that is all there was to it. And he was strict about our appearance and how we conducted ourselves on the bandstand, too. We couldn't sit sloppily or with our legs crossed, or play with cigarettes hanging from our mouths. And John made us work at all times and pay strict attention to what we were doing. Of course, he always worked hard himself and he got us to work hard that way, too. All he asked was that each one did his share to the best of his ability.

I worked just as hard under my brother as I did under anyone.

He was very strict on me and said, "Now, because you're my brother I'm not going to be any more lenient with you than anyone else." I understood that and tried to do my best to please him. But John didn't drink himself and he was always on me for my drinking. I felt I had a right to lead my own life and to drink if I wanted to, but I tried not to make him angry or to displease him in any way. But playing with John was a tough assignment for everyone. There was no outstanding individual in the outfit, everybody had to work in harmony. With a small outfit like that we either had to work together or we couldn't make music. Any criticism of the outfit was a criticism of each one of us. It made each of us aware of our own responsibility and of the need to help hold up the responsibility of the others.

John had a wonderful little outfit, and it used to please a lot of people. With only four men we played all kinds of music. It was strictly a musical band. I mean that we all read music and didn't play any head numbers. Of course if we could play the number and follow note for note without looking at the music that was all right. I could do that after I had once played a piece of music through. By improvising on the number I would make it sound better. It was really that outfit that popularized the idea of small combos. People who came to hear us didn't think a four-piece combo could do the work that we did in jazz music. It was a small outfit that was the talk of the town.

John used to call rehearsals only if somebody brought in a batch of new music. Of course he would have a rehearsal to prevent us from sitting there and blundering on the bandstand. I always hated rehearsals, though. I don't believe in preparing for things, because a person always gets it mixed up. You seldom do what you rehearse anyway. I believe in playing music the way it hits me on the spur of the moment. Sometimes John would order a rehearsal and nobody would show up but him and me. I used to drive him to the job so I was forced to be there. And when the fellows didn't come to rehearsals John would be very angry and tell them, "Well, now, since you weren't at rehearsal, you take the piece of music home with you. You'd better know it when we get together and you'd better not make any mistakes." And that's the way John was: positive, very positive.

But when he began playing saxophone we poked so much fun at

him that he refused to continue. He never took lessons on the sax but got one to use in the band. Dominique and I used to tell him that he wasn't doing so well on it. Of course, he was doing all right but we wouldn't say so. We just didn't like a sax in our outfit and wanted to hear John play clarinet. I would especially heckle him and say, "Hey, John, nobody wants that doodly, doodly, doo." Dominique used to call it the secret weapon. So he would put it down. It wasn't pleasant for him and sometimes he got very angry. But we didn't think about that; we were only thinking of the welfare of the outfit. John was very versatile and would have played sax more if we hadn't discouraged him. He didn't make a habit of not doing well and always played to the best of his ability.

John was always the leader of that outfit and he was the one who arranged for the different dates and places we played. I was happy for him to do that because I never believed that a drummer should lead a band. In my opinion a leader should carry the melody for the rest of the outfit. But a drummer hasn't got melody and can't hold anybody up. If he can't carry the melody he shouldn't be the leader. A violin, trumpet or clarinet can lead, but not the drum.

I played several engagements with John's outfit at the Three Deuces. Sam Beer owned the place and he wanted me to work for him before I went to Burt Kelly's Stables, so he nabbed me the first chance he got. There I did a two-job stunt. I played with my brother's band downstairs and then I would play upstairs with the pianist, Cleo Brown. After about three months there John left and they brought in a group led by Roy Eldridge. But after John left I only played upstairs with Cleo Brown. There wasn't any band upstairs, just Cleo and me. The Three Deuces was a kind of night spot. They brought in various entertainers like Martha Raye, Anita O'Day, Billie Holliday, and Herb Jeffries. Even Fats Waller used to come there. The place held about three hundred and fifty. And we played there with nothing but piano and drums.

Cleo would play and sing and I backed her up on drums. We never had any rehearsals and she played just as though I wasn't there. I'd follow along in my style of drumming. She used to play and sing all sorts of blues and pop numbers. She was a great gal to go around to theatres and get new show numbers to use for herself. We played only behind the bar while the customers ate and drank, not for dancing. Of course with Cleo I had to play very softly. But I still used sticks rather than brushes. I also had to hit the bass drum very lightly and tap the cymbals softly so as not to drown out her piano.

Cleo was the first girl I heard play boogie woogie. Of course I had heard that many years earlier in New Orleans. But they didn't call it boogie woogie, they called it rolling bass. And in the early days the pianists made a real number out of it and when they played they played nothing but the bass. The bass was the lead. Besides boogie woogie, Cleo had her own style of piano which was different from that of the other girl pianists I've heard. After Cleo left they got two other girl pianists. One of them, Julia Lee, was a wonderful blues singer and played fine piano, too.

I first played in the Three Deuces around 1931 and I went there again in 1938. I played upstairs behind the bar and also downstairs in the taproom they fixed up and called the Downbeat Club. For a while Natty Dominique and John were there, too, but they left for some reason and Sam Beer got Stuff Smith and Darnell Howard to replace the outfit. For a while there was violin, clarinet and drums, then they got a regular band. Then later for a short time there was only Fred Reed on the piano, Lonnie Johnson on guitar, and myself on drums. On Sundays the piano player was off and the entire outfit consisted of Lonnie Johnson and me, just guitar and drums.

Just those two instruments playing sounded very odd, and it was a very difficult routine. It was pretty hard to tone my drumming down to let just a guitar be the lead instrument. We played mostly blues and pop numbers. Lonnie was a very good guitar picker. He played the melody very nicely, and he would also sing. It was quite a thing and we used to have special people who would come out on Sundays just to hear the two of us. I would have to play along and try to do as much as I could to fill in the different parts. Then too, I had to play very softly and soothing, so as to let the guitar's sound protrude over the drum. I had to think all the time what to put in, and what not to put in. But it was a great experience and helped make me both versatile and light handed.

Even Gene Krupa couldn't see how I did it. He was playing at the Chicago Theatre and he came over and said to me, "Well, Baby, I heard about this but I didn't believe it. I came to see it. I don't see how you do it. Don't you use brushes?" I told him, no indeed, when you have to do something, you just learn how to do it, and that is all there is to that. And he would stand there and look at me and just shake his head.

I think a drummer should be versatile. A drummer can't just have one single thing in his mind. You can't go along with a one-track mind and be a good drummer. Rather, you must be thinking all the time and trying different things, different beats. And I feel a drummer should become a finished drummer. That is a drummer who has been schooled and has learned music, and his instrument.

The experience at the Three Deuces with Lonnie Johnson was a valuable one, but I almost lost my drums there in a fire. New Year's morning of 1940 a fire started in the basement in the taproom, and my drums were on the first floor behind the bar. It was just luck that the fire came in from the opposite end from my drums. The fire missed the drums and got part of the piano instead. The drums got very wet though. It was the president of the musicians' local and the superintendent of the building who got my drums out of the water. I was at home, sleeping, and didn't know anything about it until they called me and told me what had happened. The drums were at the union hall by the radiator, drying out. All I lost in the fire was one drum stick.

The Three Deuces was only one of many places where I played with John's outfit. Of course, most of the time I was there with other groups but after I left there I went to a place at Eighteenth and Indiana operated by a fellow called Pork Chops. It was a bar where they also had dancing. At that time we had, besides John and me, Natty Dominique on trumpet, Leo Montgomery on piano, and Herb Waters on tenor sax. We played the same type of music. The only difference was the addition of the tenor man. Herb Waters also did all the singing for the group and he fit in very nicely. For a period we also played for dancing at 47th and State. There it was only John, Arthur Campbell, piano, and me. It was just a rough night spot and there we also had different nights for different classes of people. That meant that we had to play different classes of music, just as at Burt Kelly's Stables. Another place where I played with John's group in the early thirties was called the Lamb's Club. It was a small cabaret with dancing. It was over on the west side around Paulina Street. It was pretty rough there. The only thing that stands out in my mind is that one little Italian fellow who used to come there pulled out a forty-five and hit my cymbal with it one night. I was scared to death. As a rule if anyone touched my drums I would yell, but not this time. But the boss came over and made the fellow apologize. He told me that if anything was broken he would pay for it and he pulled out a big roll of money. He hadn't broken anything and if he had I wouldn't have said anything. That was the only place we had trouble like that although many of the places we played were run by gangsters. We were there about five or six months. The place was misnamed. At the Lamb's Club they were really wolves in lambs' clothing.

We played at a place called the New Plantation for a while. That was also run by a gangster, a relative of Al Capone. It was closed by the law, if I remember correctly. Then there was the place called the 29 Club, run by Rocco Gallo. It was at 47th and Dearborn and mostly Negroes came there. It was the same four-piece outfit that my brother used at the other places. We played for a pretty nice floor show there and for a while King Jones, who had been the master of ceremonies at the Lincoln Gardens, was the M.C. there too.

We had about eight Negro girls in a chorus line, and there was also a comedian and a leading lady and some special acts. One fellow did a strong mouth act and another a monkey act. I had to play special drums for this show. They worked out their different acts at rehearsal and we had to furnish the kind of music they wanted. We had two rehearsals besides a dress rehearsal every week. To keep from coming back we would rehearse after the show. The show ended by six o'clock in the morning and we'd rehearse until about nine. We would also have dancing there, two shows a night and dancing in between. It was a pretty rough schedule.

After the 29 Club, John's outfit went to a place on Michigan Avenue called the Lower Deck. Al Quadback ran it and he had wanted us to play for him some time. But we didn't do so well with him and we only stayed two weeks because we weren't getting paid. The only two places where I've worked and was owed money were the Lower Deck and the New Plantation.

Around the latter part of 1934 we went to Callahan's Bar, just south of Lake Street. For a while Sterling Todd played piano and then Leo Montgomery replaced him. That left John, Leo, Natty and me. And that's the place where I lost my favorite wood block, one that I got when I worked with Oliver's band at the Gardens. There was a split in the top of it and it made the notes that came from it less piercing than before it was split. It was very large, about a foot long. And it was so heavy that without the split it almost burst your eardrums. But afterwards it was very melodious. One night I had been drinking at Callahan's Bar and I got pretty high and left my drums and everything on the stand. I generally brought them home but not that night. And that's where I lost that block. I got another one but never one with as pretty a tone as that one.

But the most difficult music I ever played was with John's little outfit at Mrs. Cohen's K-Nine Club. It was the hardest band I ever worked with and consisted of John, Leo Montgomery, Natty Dominique, Herb Waters and myself. Besides playing for dancing we had a show and the music was tough. With only five men we had to play things like *Faust,* and the *Hungarian Rhapsodies* and the like. We were there from the end of 1931 until early 1934. The K-Nine Club was really a group of fellows, female impersonators. There were only four girls in the show and the rest were fellows. They had exotic shows, and pantomimes and the music was always difficult. The fellows did a joke striptease act. I think the city closed down the K-Nine on account of the men who impersonated women. They tried to cut that sort of thing out of Chicago. I don't think they succeeded though; it's still going on. But I didn't think anything of it; it was just another job to me.

We also played at the New Stables located at Devon and Broadway and operated by a fellow named Oppenheimer. It was a much larger place than Burt Kelly's, and unlike Kelly's Stables, they had a floor show as well as dancing. That was in 1935, the year that I was sick with pleurisy. I was sick for over two weeks and Oppenheimer had already told my brother that if I didn't appear for work within a few days the whole outfit would have to leave and find another job. John didn't tell me but Dominique did and I went back to work three days after I left the hospital. That made the job stick a little longer. By that time we were well established and many people used to come in just to hear John's little outfit. It was a little sooner than I should have started working and I had to drink because I was so weak. I needed the false energy until I felt all right again.

Of course, sometimes during the depression years it was tough to get work. There weren't many jobs around but my brother was a hustler and I worried about nothing. He used to get dates to play in little taverns or saloons around town, usually on Friday and Saturday nights. There wasn't much money attached to it but still it kept the wolf away from the door. We used John's regular outfit, John on clarinet, Ralph Tervalon on piano, Natty on trumpet, and me on drums. We managed to get along all right although we never did have any other trade like so many musicians had. The Dutreys—and there were three of them: Pete, the oldest, played violin in New Orleans, Sam, who played clarinet, and Honoré, trombone—were all very good barbers as well as skilled brick masons. When music got slack they worked at those other trades. Johnny St. Cyr was a plasterer, and Natty Dominique, Manuel Perez and Freddie Keppard were cigar makers. Much later, of course, Bunk Johnson was caretaker of a large plantation, George Lewis is a stevedore, and Slow Drag Pavageau is a house painter.

Of course, John owned an apartment house at 39th and Michigan, and I got involved in a cab business with my other brother. He was my oldest brother, Bill, and he wanted something when he first came to Chicago and couldn't find work. He chose this cab business and sometimes it was confusing because both our names were W. Dodds. His was Willie and mine was Warren. He didn't have quite enough money so I put the balance in the business. John and I never drove the cabs, only William. In fact, I only drove the cab once. I left my house on 51st Street and got as far as 47th and Michigan and had an accident going across the boulevard. I never even picked up one passenger and that was the extent of my cab driving experience. Even Bill didn't drive the cabs long because the cold winters were too much for him, but we kept up the ownership of the cabs for about twenty years or more.

In those days of hard times we used to go to rent parties in Chicago. At that time rent was pretty high and we knew people who would give parties in their homes and invite all their friends. They would serve a dinner of fried chicken, chitterlings, slaw, wieners and sauerkraut, or red beans and rice. They would charge about fifty cents for such a plate dinner. Then with the money they got for the meals and drinks they paid their rent. That's why they called them rent parties. If they had music it would be no more than a piano player or maybe a three-piece outfit. Often there was a pianist and singer. That's where I heard Jimmy Yancey play quite often. I heard both Mama Yancey and Bertha "Chippie" Hill sing at such affairs. They sang and played blues and all kinds of other jazz music. Jimmy Yancey played the rolling bass style of blues piano. Jimmy used to drink pretty heavily but he was a very quiet, easy going fellow and not at all difficult to get along with.

Besides rent parties, I attended other affairs to raise money for various people. In 1937 John's little outfit participated in the benefit for Joe Sullivan given at the Congress Casino. Joe Sullivan was very ill at the time and various groups contributed their services for his benefit. Of course he had played with the Bob Crosby band so that outfit was there. And there was also a little fellow called Sugar Boy who played a piano solo. Zutty Singleton had a six-piece group there too. Our group came on right before intermission, and we were the hit of the show. The people enjoyed so much seeing us play together. Many of them had heard us play at Kelly's Stables and other places many years before. We played so much together that it sounded like six or eight instead of four. We had John, Natty, Leo Montgomery and me, and each of us had some special part. That's where I picked up the idea of doing drum solos. I did *Dinah* at the Sullivan benefit. I did thirty-two measures one time, and sixty-four another. Previously, of course, I had had solos, but they were only short things, maybe four or eight measures. But this time I had a much longer solo and it brought down the house.

Sometimes John and I would go out and play with a group of white fellows at Paul Mares' jam sessions. That was quite an experience, too, because many years before when I was just starting to play jazz music in New Orleans the white people weren't interested in it. They would laugh and poke fun at it and say it sounded crazy to them. It was music they thought was played only by illiterate Negroes. Of course, white musicians had played mostly classical music but a group of them tried to learn how to play this music. They worked in the sporting house district about half a block from where I was working. Only one of them, the piano player, knew how to read music. Since they didn't know how to read they used to mix numbers together. They only knew so much of one and so much of the other, not the whole numbers. They would play part of *Panama,* part of *Tiger*

Rag, and part of *That's a Plenty*, and put them all together. Every night they got off work first and they came by to hear us play. They picked up our numbers and played them their way. That's the way the first Dixieland band got the music. They never got the real idea of our music but played it their way. But they made a hit with it and they took jazz north to New York.

Of course the Negroes could play jazz. They didn't have an opportunity to play classical music and we'd pick up the different numbers from hearing other bands. We seldom had the money to buy sheet music. Then we'd put a little harmony in it and that's the way we played it. But the white fellows never did play jazz as well as the Negroes. They had a different environment. In fact it was only a limited group of Negroes that had it in them at all. It's not in the higher class of Negro society, but rather the next lower class. They come up whistling and dancing and singing and it's born in them. When they grew up some of them could play good jazz. But the white musicians never got organized. They could play with one or two but not with four or five. They never got together in their music. Some of them learned to read music but they didn't know how to put it together and play jazz music. They would get out of time, and lacked a sense of rhythm. Of course, you can't learn anything from someone else unless you yourself have the foundation inside you. Still, some of the white fellows learned a lot.

It was at the Paul Mares sessions where they learned some of the things. John and I were often called to Mares' place which was on State Street. We were the specials and Mares would get mostly white musicians for the rest of the group. Sometimes he played trumpet himself. The others got a big feed out of it but John and I were paid for our part. I liked it because we were hired as the special performers. Many musicians played with us in those sessions. There was Boyce Brown who played alto sax. He was a very nice fellow who was blind or nearly blind at the time. My brother especially liked him. On trombone sometimes it was Floyd O'Brien, sometimes George Brunies, and sometimes even Jack Teagarden. Once he brought his brother Charles who was just learning how to play. He hardly knew how to hold his horn, and Jack, who also plays nice trumpet, would keep at him and teach him all that he could. Of course Jack learned a lot by listening to the Negro musicians, too. Sometimes fellows from the Bob Crosby band jammed at Mares'. Bobby Haggart, Bob Zurke, Nappy Lamare, Billy Butterfield and Yank Lawson came at different times. Some of the drummers who used to come around when they were in town were Dave Tough, Gene Krupa, and George Wettling. Eddie Condon used to come with his guitar and sit in to play. Wild Bill Davison often came to those things too. Bill picked up an awful lot from these outfits. Jimmy McPartland was another one who learned a lot working at these sessions, as well as Bud Freeman with his tenor sax and Pee Wee Russell with his clarinet. Two of the pianists were Jess Stacy and Art Hodes. Mezz Mezzrow sometimes sat in too, but he was different. He had played around with Tommy Ladnier and other colored musicians years earlier. He came into the swing of his music that way.

But a lot of the fellows who later hit the big money in the swing music era learned from us oldtimers. And much of it was obtained at these Chicago sessions. My brother John blew clarinet and I kept the time steady with my drumming. We gave those fellows the time in music that they have now. In a way we gave something away. With my beat on the drums and John's keeping a perfect time with his clarinet, they couldn't go wrong. And my brother would help the others to play the melody. Naturally it put them into the swing of it. Of course, the white fellows had to be very versatile, too, in order to get the idea of the music.

A lot of drummers picked up different things from my playing. George Wettling often watched me at Lincoln Gardens and he once asked me to show him how I held my drumsticks when I worked. I showed him and for a while his drumming was very much like mine. Dave Tough used to come to listen to us at Burt Kelly's Stables and the K-Nine Club. He watched me closely, but of course, he had been drumming ever since high school, and he was already a very good drummer. Ormand Downes used to come around to the K-Nine Club, but I don't think he got any pointers from me because he knew so much himself. He's a really wonderful musician and what I call a finished drummer.[1]

Ben Pollack used to come to the Lincoln Gardens and years later I got his drums through Ray Bauduc. I knew Ray from the old days in

[1] Natty Dominique, who is very critical of drummers, stated that Downes "had a repetoire just as big as ours."

New Orleans but he used to come to watch and listen when we were playing at the Three Deuces. I think Pollack owed Ray some money, and he gave him the drums in part payment. Bauduc liked my drumming and he used to ask me how to do various things. When Pollack gave him the drums, Ray gave them to me and those were the drums which were saved when the Three Deuces burned. Gene Krupa came around for some pointers, too. When we were working at the K-Nine Club he had just got a job with Buddy Rogers' band and he wanted to know about doing show work. He couldn't see how it was possible to watch the show, the conductor, and his drums all at the same time. I told him to the best of my knowledge how it was done, and I even demonstrated the trick to him. Long before that, Gene came to Kelly's Stables and I showed him how I tuned my drums, how tight I made the heads on my snare drums and what size drumsticks I used. A lot of white musicians got ideas and pointers from me but I never really taught anyone how to drum.

One drummer wanted me to teach him when I was working with King Oliver at the Lincoln Gardens. That was Wally Bishop, who was just a little fellow then. He was still in school and his mother brought him to the Gardens and wanted me to instruct Wally. I didn't teach him though; I was too wild in those days to take on a student. But I was the inspiration of another fellow who became a very famous drummer, Zutty Singleton. His uncle, Willie Bontemps, used to bring him down to the wharf when I played on the steamer *Sidney* in New Orleans. He was still a kid in school but he used to love my drumming. He once asked his uncle, "I wonder, will I ever drum like that fellow?" I never taught Zutty a thing but I was his inspiration.

Although I never gave anyone lessons on drumming I did give one person lessons on the piano. My student was Kay Thompson.[2] I was in her house one time when she played a number for me on the piano. After she got through I pointed out where she had made a mistake. She was very much surprised that a drummer would be able to show her anything about the piano. She claimed that was a kind of help which she hadn't received from teachers before and asked me to give

---

[2]Kay C. Thompson published two interesting articles on Baby in the British magazine, *Jazz Journal:* "Baby Dodds in the role of Music Critic" (August, 1950), and "Baby Dodds in the Role of Critical Listener" (April, 1951).

her lessons. For about six months I went over to her place once a week to give her lessons on the piano. But I didn't really give her piano lessons. I only let her play and when she made a mistake in the music, I would bring her back to it. Her idol was Jelly Roll Morton. She played in his style, and did very well, too. She improved a great deal during the time I worked with her.

There were quite a few white musicians who picked up things from John's playing, too. Frank Teschmacher used to come to listen to him when we were playing on Indiana Avenue and Eighteenth Street. Pee Wee Russell used to play with John at the Paul Mares sessions in Chicago. Pee Wee tried so much to play like my brother that he did play like him for a while. And Benny Goodman used to listen to John, too. He came to the Gardens, the K-Nine Club and the New Stables. In fact he came to the Stables just before he started out on a tour with his newly organized band around 1935. He came there in tails because he had just left a big going-away dinner given in his honor. He said he wanted to hear John again before he left Chicago and he came around eleven or twelve and stayed until three or four. John put on a little extra blowing for Benny and he enjoyed it immensely. It was around that time that he had his quartet with Lionel Hampton, Gene Krupa, Teddy Wilson and himself. Soon after he left Chicago we heard the band and quartet on the radio. I don't think Benny had got my brother's playing out of his head because he sounded so much like him with the quartet. When he first started out he used to play a lot of music, a lot of music.

It was a pleasure to play with John's outfit and we played in many spots around Chicago. However, during the twenties and thirties I also played with many an outfit in Chicago without John. For a while I played with a group led by Lil Armstrong at the Dreamland at State and 35th. There we played for both dancing and shows, and we had a small outfit of about six which included Ory. I also did a lot of free lance work. I played different jobs around town with Willie Hightower. Some time around the end of 1927 I played at the Club Bagdad with an eleven-piece band led by Ralph Brown, which included three saxes and two trumpets. Archie Wahl played bass, Bud Scott, banjo, Al Wynn, trombone, and Leonard Smith, piano. Those were just some of the bands that I played with on certain weekends.

For a while I also played with Arthur Simms' eight-piece band at the Midway Gardens. That was where I fell down the elevator shaft. We had a very high bandstand and there were two doors at the back. One was to the stairway for the bandstand and the other, an abandoned elevator shaft. I opened the wrong door with my bass drum in front of me and plunged down. It made an awful racket, although my drum didn't even break. They carted me off to a white hospital at 63rd and Vernon. Instead of attending to me and giving first aid they handled me just like I was a piece of trash. Husk O'Hare was booking the band and he thought the way they treated me was terrible, and told them so. He talked to them but it didn't do any good so then he had me taken over to another hospital on Michigan Avenue where they treated Negro patients. I was only in for a short time but I had a fractured rib which had to be taped up for a while afterwards. That ended my playing with Simms, of course.

For about a year I played with Hughie Swift's band at the Evergreen Golf Club and also at the Jeffrey Tavern. At the Golf Club they had dinner music after the people got through with their golfing. We played at night during the week and on Sunday afternoons we played from about one to six. The same people owned the Jeffrey Tavern and we played there at a different time of year. We had floor shows and dancing there and we used to broadcast every Sunday. That was a large, fourteen-piece band which included Roy Palmer on trombone and Mike McKendrick on guitar and a pianist by the name of Ray Smith. Ray used to do a lot of arranging for the outfit and he made beautiful arrangements of the *Waters of Minnetonka* and *Over the Waves*. It was strictly a reading band and Hughie Swift believed in a lot of orchestration. We played them straight. It wasn't a jazz band; we'd play the music with very few changes.

The Jeffrey Tavern job was one which I messed up through drinking. Something happened at my house and I carried a strong grudge all the way from there over to 84th and Jeffrey. It was my birthday to add to it. I was very high strung and hit Hughie Swift, the leader, and almost knocked him out. Of course I lost the job and I was never so hurt in my life. It was the only time I had ever hit a fellow and I knew it was the wrong thing to do. It was very bad, too, because the musicians around Chicago were just beginning to recognize my musical ability and perhaps I could have gone much higher had it not been for my drinking. They were afraid of the responsibility. But I kept the drinking under control and never gave any trouble except that time with Hughie Swift. Swift was a very good friend, too, and afterwards he was still my friend.

Sometime around 1928 I joined the Charlie Elgar band in a peculiar way. Several of Erskine Tate's men, including his drummer, Jimmy Bertrand, left for another spot and Tate tried to get me to join his outfit. At the time Tate was playing theatres and I didn't like theatre work and didn't accept the offer. Meanwhile Charlie Elgar was playing for dancing at the Savoy and he had Zutty Singleton on drums. I loved dance music and asked if we couldn't switch and have Zutty go to Tate to play show work and have me join Elgar. Well Zutty left but I didn't join Elgar until his replacement drummer, a fellow named Christian, left the band to join the police force. Then I joined the outfit.

Elgar had a trick number which he pulled out on me the very first night. It was one they used on new men to find out if they could read music. It was about the third number and was in pencil manuscript. Of course they were all laughing about it and were sure that I would mess it up. But I played the number through, as it was written, and the whole bunch was very much surprised.

At the Savoy we had music for dancing only, but it wasn't what I would call a hot band. Elgar had a large outfit with either one or two violins and we played mostly pop tunes and semi-classics put into dance time.[3] We used to alternate with the Louis Armstrong band only it wasn't called Armstrong's band, it was called Clarence Black's Band. Of course, Louis played hot and there couldn't be two large bands of the same type. It was the first time I had played at the same place as Louis since the Oliver band broke up.

I had a tremendous variety of experiences playing in Chicago but the only time I had the contract for an outfit was on John's last job. That was at the 9750 Club and it was located on the highway going out of town. They had nothing special to attract people to the place and the fellow who used to be headwaiter at the K-Nine worked at the 9750 Club and suggested that they get a band to draw in the people who passed by. He told the manager about me and I got the

[3]In 1953 Charles Elgar, then Vice-president of Musicians Local 208 in Chicago, commented on Baby's playing: "He was an asset to the unit owing to his unique style. In the parlance of the musician he could sell the band and himself."

date under my name. Of course, I hired Natty Dominique and Leo Montgomery, which was John's regular outfit. Then they wanted to have John, too. He had been sick for two months with a stroke the previous year and was still not well. But they asked to have him come out to play only on Saturdays and Sundays and assured me that if he got sick he would not have to work. I didn't think it would hurt John to do that and I was very proud to have him there. I'd seen the time when I first started that he wouldn't even let me sit in the band with him. And after working for him for thirty years, I was able to hire him in an outfit. It was one of the biggest thrills of my musical life.

John was still pretty weak and he didn't walk so well. He wasn't crippled by his first stroke but he walked very slowly. However, I think he enjoyed working there. But in August of 1940 another stroke hit him at about ten-thirty one morning. He never regained consciousness and before noon he was gone. It was a terrible loss to all of us. We were very close as brothers and as musicians. And, as far as I'm concerned, there never was a clarinet played like my brother played. There just couldn't be another Johnny Dodds or anyone to take his place. And his passing on made a big difference in my life. I had been connected with him for many years and from then on I had to be wholly on my own.

V
Recording and Broadcasting

"The way I tried to drum required a good thinking brain and a sharp ear. And it was always necessary to keep a sense of humor, for God's sake, so that if something didn't sound right I could always change it."

I'VE MADE a lot of recordings but the biggest kick I got out of any recording session was when the King Oliver band went out to Richmond, Indiana, to record for the Gennett Company. It was in 1923 and it was my first recording experience and also the first for the rest of the band. It was something none of us had experienced and we were all very nervous. But Baby Dodds kept his nerves down in his usual way. I had a bottle and I went off and took a short intermission, and when I came back I was all set to go.

Joe Oliver got the contract through someone who had heard the band play at the Gardens and Joe decided which tunes we would record. They were all numbers which we had worked out many times on the bandstand. We journeyed from Chicago to Richmond by train and we did all that recording in one day because none of us had quarters to sleep in Richmond. We went in the morning and came back at night. Of course everybody was on edge. We were all working hard and perspiration as big as a thumb dropped off us. Even Joe Oliver was nervous; Joe was no different from any of the rest. The only really smooth-working person there was Lil Armstrong. She was very unconcerned and much at ease.

On one number I was caught very unsettled. That was *Dippermouth Blues*. I was to play a solo and I forgot my part. But the band was very alert and Bill Johnson hollered "Play that thing!" That was an on-the-spot substitution for the solo part which I forgot. And that shows how alert we were to one another in the Oliver band. The technician asked us if that was supposed to be there and we said no. However, he wanted to keep it in anyway and ever since then every outfit uses that same trick, all because I forgot my part.

On that recording date it was a small studio and we all had to be jammed together. The only ones who weren't right by the speaker were my brother John, Louis Armstrong and Dutrey. Oliver was close to the speaker. After we made the records they put them in the press right away and we heard a couple of them. It was quite a thrill to hear ourselves on wax for the first time. And in those days the records were actually processed in ovens. That's why they called them hot platters. Those records still sound to me very much like the Oliver band sounded when it played in the Lincoln Gardens.

Afterwards we recorded with Oliver's band in Chicago but that was the only trip we made to Richmond. And we had the same versatility in recording that we had when we played for dances. If anybody mentioned any novelty or anything which would improve the music we would try it. One time Joe asked Louis to bring the toy slide whistle he sometimes used in the Gardens to the recording studio. It was a novelty which helped make the band go over and Louis used it on our recording of *Sobbin' Blues*. For the most part, though, I didn't do any special parts in the Oliver recordings. Only on the record of *Someday Sweetheart** I had a little special bit. We recorded some of our very best numbers but the drumming didn't come out so well in the records of those days. It was wonderful that we got to put such things on wax as *Snake Rag, Riverside Blues* and *Canal Street Blues*.

After the Oliver band broke up I made a lot of recordings with the little outfits that John led. John used to contract with the Okeh Company and with Decca, which was then Brunswick. Quite a few of the numbers were written by members of the band. We recorded some of Lil Armstrong's music, and we used Natty Dominique's numbers pretty regularly. We also recorded quite a few of Jimmy Blythe's tunes. In fact John's band used to record for Blythe, who sometimes held the contract to make the records. Jimmy Blythe

*Gennett record: never issued (master lost or destroyed).

would demand to get John and the rest of his band. He held the contract for the records we made under the name of the Dixieland Thumpers. I only came in contact with Jimmy Blythe through those recording dates but found him a very quiet fellow, not the boisterous type at all. In appearance he was dark and short. And everything he did was always to the best of his ability. I didn't even know what outfits he played with but he played piano on the recording dates and when we used his numbers he would write out the parts and give each of us the part for our instruments.

For most of the sessions with John's outfit John used to get the contract. When we recorded for Brunswick the company would decide what numbers to record. We worked up numbers at rehearsal and then John and Jack Kapp, the person in charge of recording at Brunswick, would talk over what numbers we might put on records. Sometimes Kapp would change the numbers. Usually the other companies either gave us a list of the numbers they wanted or else took all that we had. But Brunswick was a bit more particular. Of course, they never told us how to play a number. John and the band worked that out. My brother used to take a watch and play so many choruses and ensemble or solo until the time ran out. We could never play as many choruses as we used in dances, and if there were solos they had to fit into the exact time, too. I've seen a time when we recorded a number once and were satisfied enough to let it go through without making it over. If John had any doubt about a record he would ask for the record to be played and if it didn't sound just right he would ask that the record be destroyed.

I had to make some records with John's outfit with washboard instead of drums. It was a novelty for John and for Natty Dominique but I never liked it. There wasn't anything to it, not even a tune. It was hard work, too. It worked me to death. I had never seen a washboard played but had heard about it and got some sewing thimbles to put on my fingers. But still I could feel the vibration when my fingers got to the bottom of the thimbles. After making those recordings my hands used to hurt for half an hour or more afterwards.

Of course, I always felt that John's outfit sounded better in person than on the records we made. Hearing recordings is never just like seeing the musicians play. I could never understand how the record business made such a big hit because people that heard the music heard it plain without knowing the personnel. It makes quite a difference when you see the musicians and get to know them as people rather than just hear them on records.

But people wanted the records and we were glad to make them. We got paid well but it was tough work recording in the day and playing for dancing at night. We were on the go all the time. While we rehearsed the music in the recording studio we were not paid but when the technician held his hand up to signal that a master was made, that was your money. Each musician got thirty dollars a side. Sometimes we made records all week, and, of course, we played music every night, too. Working during the day didn't spare us at night. We had to go on the job and work just as hard. In the studios the air was tight and we worked hard to play through one horn or mike. When we came out we were tired. But we didn't have time to go home and eat, lie down and relax or sleep, we had to go right on and jump out of those sweaty clothes, and get into our dress clothes to go to work. Then many a time we had to report the next morning at eight o'clock for more recording.

In the spring of 1927 John and I made some recordings with Louis Armstrong's Hot Seven. With Louis' outfit we used to have rehearsals and anything that we had in mind for any particular number we would work out then. He would tell each of us when to take a solo or when not to, and who would come in at different times. We weren't a bunch of fellows to write down anything. That would have made it too mechanical. We would stop and talk it out more than anything else. If there was any writing involved, Lil would write down what the musicians were supposed to do. Of course we all had our ideas to give the band, and we would work them out at rehearsal. Later we rehearsed the number again in the recording studio. Whenever a fellow wanted to change something he would ask Louis for his opinion and if it was agreeable it was in. But Louis allowed each of us to take a lot of responsibility for those records. If I would even ask him a question about playing he'd say "Ah go ahead, you know what to do." That made us responsible and gave us plenty of leeway to use our own ideas. The only thing that Louis demanded was that we worked to do our best on the records.

Sometimes when recording with Louis I used the afterbeat cymbal to back him up. I used this on the record we made of *Willie the*

Weeper. It was my style of playing and I used it often for dancing. Some people today think that my drumming was heavy; it wasn't that at all, but rather it was because my technique was so sharp. Each time I hit the cymbal it was clear and distinct, but it wasn't that I was hitting it hard. I was careful to try to hit the cymbal or rims, or even the woodblock, just right, and the way I tried to drum required a good thinking brain and a sharp ear. And it was always necessary to keep a sense of humor, for God's sake, so that if something didn't sound right I could always change it or quickly insert something else in its place.

With Louis' recording outfit we used four beats to the measure. That was different from the older days in New Orleans when we always used two. King Oliver used two, also. And Louis used a tuba instead of a string bass. I had started playing with a bass viol and always felt closer to it than to a tuba. It was no harder to drum with a tuba but it always made the group sound brassy to me. It seemed like it was a brass band or a street band. Jelly Roll Morton also used a tuba on his records.

One time there was a little incident on a Louis recording session in connection with my drinking. It was a time when I had been drinking and forgot to report to the Brunswick studio. I had rehearsed for the session but when the time came to make the records John had a hard time finding me. Finally he located me at home and I hurried over to the studio. Jack Kapp and my brother got in a huddle and John told Kapp that I had been drinking so Kapp told me he didn't want anything like that in his studio. He was very strict about the musicians drinking while they recorded for him. And of course that pleased John, who never drank himself and always objected to my drinking. I had a bottle in my coat pocket and I tried to steal a drink while they weren't looking. I had the stopper out and was just about to take a drink when they started to play so I quickly hid the bottle behind the bass drum. But the bottle dropped and broke and they heard the noise and smelled the whiskey. All heads turned in my direction and I got a slight bawling out for that, but it didn't amount to very much.

John and I also made records with Jelly Roll Morton's Red Hot Peppers. On all the jobs with Jelly Roll it was he who picked the men for the session. He went around himself and got the men he wanted to record with him. We weren't a regular band but—like Louis' Hot Seven—only a recording outfit. Sometimes the various men in the band wouldn't see each other for months. But when Jelly Roll gave us a ring we met for rehearsal and we all knew what was expected of us. Of course we all knew each other from New Orleans but those record sessions were the only times we all got together to play music. But there was a fine spirit in that group and I enjoyed working with Jelly Roll immensely. We were always happy to see each other in the outfit and to sit down and talk over what had happened since we last got together.

At rehearsal Jelly Roll Morton used to work on each and every number until it satisfied him. Everybody had to do just what Jelly wanted him to do. During rehearsal he would say, "Now that's just the way I want it on the recording," and he meant just that. We used his original numbers and he always explained what it was all about and played a synopsis of it on the piano. Sometimes we had music and he would mark with a pencil those places which he wanted to stand out in a number. It was different from recording with Louis. Jelly didn't leave much leeway for the individual musician. You did what Jelly Roll wanted you to do, no more and no less. And his own playing was remarkable and kept us in good spirits. He wasn't fussy, but he was positive. He knew what he wanted and he would get the men he knew could produce it. But Jelly wasn't a man to get angry. I never saw him upset and he didn't raise his voice at any time. He wasn't hard to please and after making a record he would let us know when he was pleased with it.

Although Jelly used to work out all the different parts himself, he often gave us something extra to do, some little novelty or something. When we made the *Jungle Blues* he wanted a gong effect and I think I used a large cymbal and a mallet to produce the effect he wanted. One number that was pretty complicated for me was Jelly's *Billy Goat Stomp*. There were places in that where the vocalist made a noise like a billy goat and I had to do something else on the drums at the same time. It was in Spanish rhythm like so many of the numbers used to be played in New Orleans. I used the cymbal and soft mallet on that number and also the Chinese tom-tom. Another tricky one was the *Hyena Stomp*. It took quite a bit of rehearsing on some of those to get just what Jelly wanted but he told us what he expected and we would do our best to get the right effect. I was very versatile then and picked up the idea when Jelly played it on the piano. He was pleased with John's playing and with my drumming. And the records we made with Jelly were made under the best of recording conditions. They were recorded in the Chicago Victor studio on Oak Street near Michigan Avenue, and the acoustics there were very good. It was one of the best studios I ever worked in.

Besides making records with Jelly's band John and I also made trio records with him. They were also Jelly Roll's tunes and most of them he had previously recorded as piano solos. He added the clarinet and drum parts but he didn't want these other instruments to stand out. He just wanted to feel us, not to hear us. Because he wanted the drum so very soft I used brushes on *Mr. Jelly Lord*. I didn't like brushes at any time but I asked him if he wanted me to use them and he said "Yes." So I played the whole number with brushes instead of sticks. On the same number he wanted John to play only in the low register, and that's the way he played it. It wasn't John's version, but rather the way Jelly wanted him to play. On the *Wolverine Blues* I decided to try using my Chinese tom-tom. I figured it would change the beat yet still sound good, and Jelly left it in the record.

When he made those trio recordings Jelly patted his foot to keep his tempo. He was so determined about his time that he stamped his foot. It was his tempo but if we followed it we would be off and of course he didn't like that. Once the technician said that Jelly stamped his foot so loud it sounded like two bass drums. In order to keep it from the recording they had a little mattress made, about eight inches square, which they put under his foot so he could stamp all he wanted to and yet not be heard. The trio idea was Jelly's and it was something new for records. It was through this trio of Jelly, John and I that a lot of people got the idea and jazz trios became a popular thing.

The last recordings I made with John was in June of 1940 in the Chicago Opera House. The Decca Company wanted a band to play the old New Orleans type of music and most of the men on that date were from New Orleans. John played clarinet, Natty Dominique played trumpet, Preston Jackson, trombone, Lonnie Johnson, guitar, Johnny Lindsay, bass, and Richard M. Jones, piano. Only we called him Myknee Jones instead of Richard. The numbers we recorded were *Gravier Street Blues* and the *Red Onion Blues*. There was another band in the studio making another part of the Decca set and Jimmie Noone and Tubby Hall played with that outfit. Preston Jackson, Natty, Johnny Lindsay and Myknee Jones also played with that group.

I hadn't made records for quite a number of years before that and John had just had all his teeth taken out. He was worried about his playing and didn't think it sounded right. But John sounded wonderful and he was feeling very much up to par on the date. He had no teeth but his lip was in perfect shape. He was a lip man and a lot of his staccato was lip work. But John didn't have to work seriously to develop his playing, it was just in him to be the clarinet player that he was. And on those records he had the same fine tone which he had when he first started playing clarinet nearly thirty years earlier.

The first recording I did after John's death was with an outfit led by Sidney Bechet. Sidney had a contract and he wanted to record a number in memory of John, which he called *Blues For You, Johnny*. He thought it would be nice to have me on drums so he looked me up in Chicago. I had played with him years earlier in New Orleans but never since I had gone to Chicago. I hadn't drummed since John had died, about a month earlier, and I was a bit nervous. I hadn't practiced but picked up my drumming where I had left off. The records were made under the name of Sidney Bechet and his New Orleans Feetwarmers and I thought they sounded very nice. Besides Sidney and myself, the musicians were Rex Stewart on trumpet, Earl Hines on piano, and Johnny Lindsay on bass. Herb Jeffries took the vocal on *Blues For You, Johnny*. It was a fine tribute from Sidney since he and John had been friends and had come up together in New Orleans. Later I made some records with Mezzrow and Bechet. They harmonized together very well. There was no brass on those records, just soprano sax, clarinet, piano, bass and drums.

I also made some other records with trios and very small groups besides the ones we made with Jelly. Early in 1944 I made four numbers with the pianist, Tut Soper. They were made for John Steiner and I got a big kick out of them. Two years later I made some records with Freddy Shayne and with a small group backing up Bertha "Chippie" Hill, the blues singer. On one of the Freddie Shayne sides I used the rims of my drums for the second chorus. I didn't have that worked out ahead of time but as I played I watched his way of playing and tried to come in with something that would correspond to it on the drums. It is almost a routine which you feel rather than think about. Freddie Shayne is a very good piano player and I wanted to have him and Lee Collins and Chippie Hill go to New York with me as a jazz group. I still think it would have been a grand outfit and a big hit. But Lee and Freddie decided to stay on in Chicago and Chippie Hill went to New York with Rudi Blesh booking her. Later in New York I played a number of dates with Chippie and small outfits. Sometimes we had Edmond Hall on clarinet and sometimes Garvin Bushell. We had a small job at the Village Vanguard with Edmond Hall, clarinet, and Sammy Benskin on piano. I never did get that outfit organized but I still think it was a good idea.

However, in December of 1945 I was able to contract with an outfit for making records under my own name. It was for Blue Note and came about through my friendship with Alfred Lion, owner of the company. He had promised that someday he'd give me a chance to have my own group on some recordings and I got quite a kick out of being the head of the outfit. We had Albert Nicholas on clarinet, Art Hodes on piano, and Wellman Braud on bass. We only had one rehearsal in the studio and I was actually in the background. My name was on the contract but I didn't tell anyone how to play or even what to play. The other fellows suggested numbers to record and we tried them out and then recorded them. Of course, as leader I felt that it was my place to let everybody else have a showing. By the time my chance came it was all over and the recording was finished. But I didn't care about that. I was interested in being the leader and having my name on the records.

About a month afterwards I made some more records under my own name, this time with a trio for the Circle Company. Rudi Blesh chose the personnel which included Albert Nicholas on clarinet and Don Ewell on piano. Nicholas played very well and we recorded one of his own numbers, *Albert's Blues.* We also made a version of Jelly Roll Morton's *Wolverine Blues* which I had recorded with Jelly nearly twenty years before. Don Ewell played a lot in the style of Jelly and I thought he did very well. However, he wasn't satisfied. It was his first recording and he thought that he was not relaxed enough. I told him if that's what comes from being tense he should feel that way all the time, because I was very happy with his playing on that record. The trio recorded an old New Orleans number, *Buddy Bolden's Blues,* on the same date. I made another record with just Don Ewell and myself. It was his own number which he called *Manhattan Stomp.* We didn't rehearse it. He played the piano and I just followed.

In 1947 I made some recordings with another trio consisting of Art Hodes, Pops Foster and myself. They were made in New York, too, but I didn't like them so well. The music was all right but there was something wrong with the setting and recording and they didn't sound right to me. A year before that I had made other records with Art Hodes which were supposed to be part of a history of jazz series. It was an idea of Miss Sheelagh Dille, who asked Art Hodes to get a group together to make recordings which would show jazz history. There was one group which I had and another which Pops Foster led. The records we made were like the early days in New Orleans when two bands would meet and have a contest in the street. After Pops' outfit would play a number there would be some talking between the musicians and some one would say "Oh, you haven't got any band. You ought to hear this Baby Dodds' band. Pops Foster, Baby Dodds is going to run you out of town." Then, of course, my outfit would let loose with another number. It was a very nice history of New Orleans jazz which we put on records.[1]

We really made jazz history in 1944, however, when I recorded with Bunk Johnson's band. It was for Bill Russell's American Music label and Bill chose the musicians. The men were all New Orleans musicians and Bunk was the only one whom I had ever played with before, although I had known Billy Marrero, the bass player, and the father of Lawrence, who played banjo in Bunk's outfit. It was the first time in many years that I had heard Bunk. The last time I had worked with him was around 1916, twenty-eight years earlier. He sounded very good. I was quite surprised to hear him play so well after all those years. I could tell a difference in his playing though. His experience told. He didn't attack his notes as roughly as he had before and he was more technical about it. Of course, when he was younger he had more power. He always could read very well so that

---

[1]The history of jazz sides were never issued but an interesting description of them written by Art Hodes appeared in *The Jazz Record,* No. 50 (November, 1946), p. 8.

aspect didn't improve any. But Bunk's playing smoothed out an awful lot in those years.

On one of those records I even took a vocal. There was a fellow who came in off the streets and sang a blues,[2] and he also brought a bottle off the street with him. Bill didn't know about the bottle and I wasn't supposed to drink at all on account of my poor health. But I caught some of the bottle and that put me in a mood to sing. I told Bill I'd like to sing a number and he probably thought I suddenly got ambition and said "All right, go ahead." It was a blues song but we played it too fast for real blues. I sang while I drummed the number. They were playing the blues so I put words to it as I went along. I had sung some in earlier outfits. Louis and I used to take vocals on the riverboats and sometimes I sang with the Hughie Swift band, with Mike McKendrick. Bill called the number *Listen to Me*. I never thought much of it—that is, of the vocal part of the record.

About a year later, in May of 1945, Bill Russell had us record some numbers with Bunk Johnson's brass band. It was like music I used to play for New Orleans parades when I was just starting to play and recording it put me back in the same mood I had years ago. On those sides I played the snares and Lawrence Marrero played bass drum. It was a wonderful experience and brought back a lot of memories. Those records were made out of doors in George Lewis's backyard. The following year I made some brass band sides for Rudi Blesh's Circle label. They sounded a little different because they were recorded in a studio in the Godchaux Building in New Orleans. It was in that building where they didn't want Negroes in the recording studio. Rudi Blesh was writing a column for the *New York Herald Tribune* at the time and he threatened to give them a write-up if they didn't permit us to make the records. We didn't know what it was all about until we got there but they finally allowed us to make our records. On that same date we made some records with a small outfit, the Eclipse Alley Five, which included Jim Robinson, George Lewis, Lawrence Marrero, Slow Drag Pavageau and myself. I didn't care for those sides at the time, although they didn't sound so bad after I heard them on records.

I also made some records in New York with Bunk's outfit. In November of 1945 we made four sides for Decca and the next month

[2]The singer was Ed "Noon" Johnson, and the number, *Do Right Baby*.

eight numbers for Victor. I wasn't so pleased at the way they muffled my drums on the Victor recordings. They placed a small mattress against the head of the bass drum and put a bucket of sand against that. Of course it made a perfect muffler. And that's why you don't hear much of my drums on those recordings. I had padded my drums on records before—sometimes I put Pops Foster's waterproof bass viol case beside my bass drum to cut down the sound—but I had never muffled it to that extent.

The following month we made some records with Sister Ernestine Washington, the spirituals singer, and I really enjoyed that session. She is a fine sacred music singer and sounded so good because the band played so wonderfully behind her. I especially enjoyed it because the way we were placed around the studio I could hear every instrument distinctly. The band was playing at the Stuyvesant Casino at the time and it sounded so much better in that studio. At the Stuyvesant we were in a big, open hall and in the studio we were in a rather small room. There it sounded more like a group than we did in the dance hall and that was partly why I got such a big kick out of making those four records.

In 1947, while I was broadcasting on Rudi Blesh's "This is Jazz" program, I made some records from the broadcast. I had also done some broadcasting years before, in 1927 when I played with Hughie Swift's band in Chicago's Jeffrey Tavern. We had a special broadcast show worked out which took a half hour every week. It was a large band and we had special numbers and arrangements for the broadcast. We played semi-classical numbers like *Waters of Minnetonka* and *Missouri Waltz*, which our piano player, Ray Smith, arranged for the outfit. We broadcast immediately after Guy Lombardo, who was then at the Granada at 67th and Cottage Grove. It was a very nice show but we didn't play hot jazz or any rowdy numbers, mostly pops and semi-classics. Sometimes I used to sing some of the pop numbers. I sang duets with the guitar player, Mike McKendrick, and some numbers he sang alone.

I never sang on the "This is Jazz" broadcasts but the music we played there was hot jazz. I had been working around New York doing concert jobs and jam sessions and mentioned to Rudi Blesh that I thought it would be a nice thing to have a band get together to broadcast. They could make a show out of it like other shows in New

York. Rudi thought it was a good idea and he got the Mutual Broadcasting Company to sponsor the show. The band we got consisted of both white and Negro musicians. Many of them were from New Orleans, including Edmond Hall, Albert Nicholas, George Brunies, Danny Barker, Pops Foster and myself. It was a little different from the New Orleans style but I enjoyed it. For a while we had Muggsy Spanier and at other times Wild Bill Davison playing trumpet. We worked pretty hard and for the most part had a lot of good feeling though it was a band that only got together for broadcasts. Every Friday we rehearsed for an hour or hour and a half. We had special feature artists on the shows too. We featured Louis Armstrong, Bertha "Chippie" Hill and James P. Johnson at different times.

It was Rudi Blesh's show, he chose the musicians and picked the tunes we played. He told us pretty much what he wanted and how he wanted it done, but he was very easy to get along with as a director. Sometimes I had solos, but they were just slight, little things, not big. I loved to play for those broadcasts. It's a grand feeling to know that you're playing for the world to hear. And we always had a packed studio. That made it very nice. It is much more satisfying than playing to an empty place like a recording studio.

Rudi didn't want us to drink at rehearsals or on the broadcast and once I had a little incident because of that. Somebody brought a bottle to rehearsal and, of course, George Brunies and I got some of it. That was all right but on the way home I stopped at every saloon I could see and that night I didn't finish. I drank on through the night and the next day I wasn't feeling so good. When broadcast time came I was asleep and when I woke up and turned on the radio I heard the "This is Jazz" program. I jumped out of bed and ran down to the studio and heard the last part of the show from the technician's booth. I felt very bad to have gone through the rehearsing and then to sit and look while the bunch was playing. That's what hurt. Blesh had got Freddie Moore to take my place on the show. He was very angry with me. For a fact, I was fired for a minute. Of course I came back and I felt like a little boy that had been up to mischief and his mother had allowed him to come back home. I was just the same as a kid at school with a dunce cap on his head. I was very careful with everything I did and felt very sheepish. A lot of people were there and of course when I came back they wanted to know what had happened. Naturally I couldn't say; all I could say was that I was sick. That "sick" business covers a lot of territory.

I made some other records for Rudi Blesh in 1947. That was with Tony Parenti's Ragtimers, a pickup outfit, but the best of its kind that we played with. Rudi and Tony Parenti chose the men for those records and Tony picked the numbers. The idea was to record the old style music—ragtime or syncopation—and Parenti, as the leader, told each of us what we should do, what numbers we would play, what tempos we would play them in and when we would have our breaks. For the most part he didn't write it out but talked it out at rehearsals. We had two different rehearsals for about an hour each. Some of the parts were written down but not mine. I just followed along. Of course Parenti was from the old school in New Orleans and he wanted to revive the kind of music they played in his young days. And he succeeded rather well. The music sounded all right. I didn't have any special or stand-out part on those records but I was happy to make them because I knew Tony Parenti wanted me especially because I knew the type of music he wanted us to play.

My favorite number from that session was one called *Hiawatha*. I liked it because it brought back so many memories of my early days. I had heard it played many times by brass bands in New Orleans when I was just a little tot. They used to play it in street parades and at the Mardi gras and I hadn't heard it since I was a child. Another number we recorded was a Tony Parenti original which he called *Praline*. I had never heard the number before that session, but it was named for a type of pecan candy I knew as a kid. We called it plarine.

Very shortly after the Parenti records I made some others with Mutt Carey and his New Yorkers. Mutt Carey had the contract, he chose the men and the tunes. He also directed the session and told us how many choruses we would play, and what we should or shouldn't do on each one. It was also all talked out. But the men were individualists and, though it was a nice outfit, we weren't together long enough to understand how to play together. We only had one rehearsal and that was in the studio. They played well, but I didn't have the understanding of the men that I like to have when I play. Musicians should really understand each other like a man and wife. Your wife can look at you and you understand what she means. You can say only one word and she will understand. Well, that's the way an organization of musicians should be. One guy can say something and everybody ought to understand. That makes for harmony in the group, and to really understand one must study each and every person until he knows what will bring contentment or discontent. I never had a chance to do this with the Mutt Carey outfit because of the short time we played together.

About four years after making the Mutt Carey records I attended a New York recording session for some youngsters who called themselves the Dixieland Rhythm Kings. I didn't play with them but they wanted me to be there while they recorded. They sounded very good although the drummer was drumming on the wrong side of the bass drum. I corrected him and all of them were interested in learning more about playing jazz music. It was a good feeling to know that these young musicians wanted me there and that I was an inspiration to them.

In 1946 I made a series of drum solos which was really a new experience for me. Some were made for Disc and some for Circle but the original idea was Frederic Ramsey's. When he talked to me about it I considered it a pretty good idea. It was just another job. Some of them were just the drum parts of standard numbers. Those were *Careless Love* and *Maryland, My Maryland,* which were both very familiar to me. I played them just as I would have with a band but on *Careless Love* I used brushes just to see what it would sound like all alone.

It was my idea to make drum solos of those two numbers but the other solo records were originals. When the lights came on they asked me what I was going to do and I told them I didn't know. They told me to go ahead and work it out my own way. When I had finished each number they asked what I wanted to name it and I gave them a name for each one as I went along. I didn't plan anything for fear that I wouldn't carry out just what I had planned. That would throw the whole thing off. And, of course, none of the solos were rehearsed. But I liked those solos very much. To tell the truth about it I was as much surprised as anyone else. I had never done solo work like that and it was very difficult because I had no melody to follow. I had drums alone and nothing else to help out.

My favorite drum solo was the one I called *Improvisation Number*

Two. I especially liked it because of the changes in it and the different tempos. As with my other solos I had a sort of blueprint in my mind but I had to think the number out as I went along. And in this number I used the rims of my snare drum to get the effect I wanted.

I also liked the *Tom-Tom Workout* very much. I made that with only three tom-toms and used the snare drum for my fourth. The snare drum was my pilot or lead on that record. Like the other solos, that one was never written down. I remember it well but am not even sure that I could write it out. I named another one of the solos *Spooky Drums* because making those records was the spookiest thing I had ever done in my life. It felt very peculiar to be in a big studio with no other performer in there but myself. And when I made this number it just struck me that hearing such sounds late at night would be very spooky. If you heard drums late at night beating that sort of beat, why my God, you'd run yourself to death.

I named one solo *Nervebeats* because it was something I had in mind which caused a lot of nervous tension. A beat like that with two sticks comes from the nerves and really is a nervebeat. This was one of the ideas which I had in mind and worked out on that session. I got the idea for the *Rudiments* number from my playing in so many different bands. I would try something different with each outfit in which I played. What might work out well with one group would not fit or sound good with another. That's my theory about playing drums and it is why I worked out so many different rhythms in my work. I named the number *Rudiments* because it was the rudiments which I would use playing with a band. The rudiments could be used with any number but instead of saying "I used this with King Oliver, and this with Louis," I just called the number *Rudiments*.

VI
Later Years

"I never worried about the instrumentation of any outfit but thought rather of who was in it and what they were doing. You worry about the harmony in the group."

I HADN'T PLAYED with Jimmie Noone since around 1914 when I was just beginning to play in New Orleans. Although my brother and the fellows in Kid Ory's band wouldn't let me sit in with them, Jimmie used to allow me to play with his band. His drummer was a Creole fellow named Arnold de Pass and he sometimes let me play his drums in the band. That was a long time ago, and it wasn't until the latter part of 1941 that I played with Noone once again. It seems that several people had asked Noone to get me to play drums and he thought it was a pretty good idea so he asked me to join his outfit. At first he wasn't too sold on the idea of hiring me because, like my brother, he didn't drink and he didn't allow anybody around him to drink, not while they were playing music, anyway.

Jimmie Noone was a pretty easy-going fellow. And when he hired a person he figured he was capable and he would let him use his own judgment in playing. Instead of telling us how to play a number he'd say, "Well, you know how to do it. Use your own judgment." Well, that gave you a chance to relax and play with Jimmie. Jimmie wasn't a hard fellow to play with. He was relaxed himself and he wanted you to be the same way. If a musician came into the outfit all excited he'd say, "Don't get excited. Relax." I never saw Jimmie Noone angry once in my life, not once.

Jimmie's playing was very good, too. The clarinet isn't supposed to carry melody in a jazz band, it's supposed to weave in and out. But Jimmie would carry the melody. Actually, he played more like a fellow would play a violin. And then with the little weaving in and out that he did, he would touch it off a bit. He was a straight clarinet player but he also played jazz. He played much as the other Creole clarinetists used to play in New Orleans.

Jimmie Noone's little band consisted of only four players. Mada Roy played piano, Jimmie, clarinet, Bill Anderson, bass, and I played drums. Even in New Orleans Noone hadn't had a trumpet in his band except for a short while when he had Sugar Johnny playing with him. The sound of the outfit was different from the others I played with but to me it was just another job of playing music. I never worried about the instrumentation of any outfit but thought rather of who was in it and what they were doing. You worry about the harmony in the group. In that outfit it was very good but I stayed with Noone only a short time. We played at a club for dancing about three months and then he got a contract to go to California. I didn't want to leave Chicago at the time so I left the Noone outfit.

Actually, most of the jobs I had from 1940 until 1944 were freelance jobs. When John lived he used to get all the contracts and after he died I didn't try to go out and get a regular job. During those years I played only for dancing at various dances and taverns. The taverns used to stay open until six o'clock and they hired bands on different nights to pull the crowd along. I played with a lot of little outfits, but none of them regularly.

Sometimes I played in jam sessions sponsored by Harry Lim at the Hotel Sherman. Of course the outfits varied from time to time and those sessions were never rehearsed at all. One time at a jam session at the Congress Casino in Chicago I used a novelty I had worked out using two sticks and my foot to play a solo on my tom-tom. I used to do *Tea for Two* and *Dinah* with that method. I put my foot on the head of the tom-tom and got different tones by moving my foot around in different places. That way I could change the tonation of the tom-tom. I think I worked that out while working with Laura Rucker at Tin Pan Alley. While there I used to do different little things for the novelty. Well, I took the idea and pulled it on the bunch at this jam session. They were very much surprised since I had never used it at any jam session before. I enjoyed it and it made a very good showing.

I worked out another little novelty using three tom-toms and the snare. I took a soft mallet and played *When the Saints Go Marching In* using only the four drums. Those tom-toms were tuneable and before playing the number I would tune them so as to get just the right pitch. I worked that out while playing with Art Hodes and Cecil Scott at Ryan's on 52nd Street in New York. I worked these different novelties out in my head before I tried them but I never practiced them. I played from what I had figured would be the thing to do and just started into it when I felt it would sound right.

I got those three tom-toms just before going to New York to play with the Bunk Johnson outfit. I had used tom-toms before but never in a set. I had only used one little Chinese tom-tom. But I got the idea for using three tom-toms from seeing a picture in a paper of Gene Krupa's drum set. I never heard him play them but I thought it was a good idea so I got a set for myself. Then I found out that they were very tuneable so I tuned them to get the tone I wanted. The first time I used them was playing with Bunk.

That job came to me through Bill Russell who had been a good friend to John. When he was trying to get the Bunk Johnson band together in 1944 he came and asked me if I would like to go down and play with them in New Orleans for some recordings. It had been many years since I had heard Bunk and I didn't even know that he was still living. In the old days I used to drink quite a bit with him, and how he could drink! He used to be quite a wine drinker but he would drink anything. Of course he couldn't drink like he used to when I met him again. And neither could I. I was sick with high blood pressure before I left Chicago and when I went to New Orleans I was only allowed to drink pineapple juice. I had also become very stout, weighing around a hundred and eighty-five which was too much weight for a small frame like mine. And I took sick after my return to Chicago, too. In fact, I have been sick ever since and haven't stopped taking pills and pills and tablets and pills, since then.

In that Bunk band we had Bunk on trumpet, George Lewis, clarinet, Jim Robinson on trombone, Lawrence Marrero, banjo, Slow Drag Pavageau, bass, and myself on drums. Most of the fellows in the Bunk Johnson band had played together under George Lewis before they joined Bunk. George is a very quiet, meek sort of fellow who never liked to squabble with anyone. George is a real natural clarinet player and he works hard and gives the band all he's got. And on one of my trips to New Orleans in 1946 I played a date with George's outfit below New Orleans, Point à la Hache.

I made several trips between Chicago and New Orleans in 1944 and 1945, and September 1945 I played with Bunk Johnson's band in the Stuyvesant Casino in New York. It was the first time I had been to New York and I loved it very much. The Stuyvesant was a dance hall and some people came to dance and some just to listen. It was really astonishing for some of the people in New York to hear the sort of music that we played, especially to hear it played by a group that was really from New Orleans. That's what made it such a big hit. All kinds of people came to listen to our band. When I first went to New York it seemed very strange to have people sitting around and listening rather than dancing. In a way it was similar to theatre work. But it was peculiar for me because I always felt as though I was doing something for the people if they danced to the music. It never seemed the same when they just sat around and listened. We played for dancing and quite naturally we expected people to dance. That was even true of our records and today some folks dance to the recordings we made.

In New York I tried different things with my drums that I had wanted to work out for a long time before. I varied my drumming from time to time. One night I would drum one way and the next night a different way. Sometimes I would use the wood block more, and again some nights I would beat more on the cymbal. Some nights I would use the rims and at other times I would put more work on the snare drums. I'd just change it around from time to time. But with my bass drum I always used what Natty Dominique calls my forty-five degree beat. That is, I always drew up my ankle to about a forty-five degree slant when I hit the bass drum foot pedal. Some drummers don't bring their foot up high enough and instead of a distinct clear beat they get a rumble effect. But I always wanted a sharp beat whenever I hit that bass drum. And this I did with all the outfits in which I played throughout my whole career.

While in New York I, of course, heard other bands, but none of them playing there in 1945 played our style of music. It was a completely different way of playing. Now they're trying to study this old style and they are beginning to play the way we had always been used to. None of the other musicians sat in with the Bunk Johnson group because they didn't know how to play the style that we played. It was just so different that they couldn't do it.

When I was with Bunk Johnson he didn't allow us to go around and play with other fellows. We were to sit in with no one but our own group. Of course I used to slip off and play with other outfits anyway. I sat in once or twice with Muggsy Spanier who was then playing at Nick's. I also used to go to Eddie Condon's place and sit in with his outfit. When Bunk took the whole outfit someplace, of course, we all went along to play. Once we played a concert at Carnegie Hall and Milton Berle was our stage announcer. I had known him from Chicago where he used to come around to the Stables when they featured theatrical night. I think that James P. Johnson and Clarence Williams played solos at the concert. I played with Bunk's band and also had a solo number which went over very big.

After playing with Bunk's band for several months I returned to Chicago, but stayed only six months before going back to New York. There I had to wait a six months period before I could get a union card and then I got a job playing with Art Hodes in a cabaret on Broadway. He had George Lugg playing trombone, Henry Goodwin on bass, and, of course, Art Hodes played piano. That was a mixed band, all were colored except Art and George Lugg. Later I played with Art Hodes at Ryan's but there we had only three instruments, piano, clarinet and drums. Art Hodes, Cecil Scott and I played there for about a year. We played pop numbers and such standards as *Maple Leaf Rag* as best we could with only three men. But the group sounded very good. We would play for about half an hour and then had a piano to relieve us for a half hour before we went on again.

I also used to play in jam sessions while I was in New York. Sometimes these were sponsored by Bob Maltz and at other times by Jack Crystal. They were mixed groups and hired for each occasion. I wouldn't know who was going to be playing in the band until I got on the job. I played several times with Joe Sullivan, Max Kaminsky, Pops Foster, and Pee Wee Russell, and sometimes with James P. Johnson. They were very happy when I went to play with them and I never had any trouble getting along with these outfits. Of course, such jobs are not as satisfactory as playing regularly with the same outfit. There couldn't be the same understanding that men have who all belong to the same group and play together every night. With a regular band you could get to know the temperament of each man playing and that's very important when playing together. But it was a very nice thing to get together and these mixed jam sessions have made New York a very popular place among white and colored musicians.

While we were playing in jam sessions the various musicians would indicate who would be taking solos. They would work that out as they went along. I never had a chance to study each player as well as I would have liked but still I tried to adapt my drumming to each player. I had to study the individuals as I went along and do things that I thought would make him work. I would have something in mind as a musician went into a solo. And if I found that what I planned didn't seem to work out so well, I'd try something else. I tried my best to work to the advantage of every player. It was hard work because I never knew exactly what the other players would do or what would be best until we actually got into a number. But all the men worked very hard at those jam sessions and lots of them played very smoothly together.

In New York I also had a somewhat different job one time when I played drums for a dance recital given by Merce Cunningham. He had heard of my drumming and one day he came to the place where I was living and asked me to play something on the drums. I told him I didn't know what he wanted and he asked me to just start drumming. When I began he said, "That's what I want. I'll work out a routine to that." He asked me if I would be willing to play alone and I told him it made no difference to me. It was just like playing a show, when you've played one show you've played them all. We had only one rehearsal and that was for about an hour and a half the day before the show. I had never seen dancing just like that before and still don't know exactly what he was trying to represent.

At the Merce Cunningham recital we did that one number with only drums and the dance. It was something like my solo work but, of course, there was someone else I had to keep up with. Sometimes I'd have to hit the cymbal on the jumps and on the turns I would make a roll. Of course the dance was all his idea and I didn't know exactly what he would do next. That's like other shows, too, because you can never depend on what an actor will do. He may do something altogether different from what he rehearsed if he thinks it will make the act go over. That is, if he's versatile. And I had to be versatile enough to change with them. But I followed Merce Cunningham's routine quite easily. That came naturally to me. When you have drummed as long as I had you just sort of feel those things. You don't have to know exactly what you're going to do but it just works out that way. I got a big kick out of playing for that dance recital and the number went over very big, too.

From Ryan's I went to Europe for eight weeks in the spring of 1948. Mezz Mezzrow was taking a group to Europe and he came and asked if I would like to make the trip and I told him yes. The band included Bob Wilber on clarinet and soprano sax, Henry Goodwin, trumpet, Jimmy Archey, trombone, Sammy Price on piano, and Pops Foster on bass. We were supposed to tour quite a bit of Europe but we only got to tour France. We played in Paris and Nice and then in the northwestern section of the country.

In Europe we played the same sort of music we used to play in the States and those people really loved it. We played numbers like *High Society, Muskrat Ramble, Panama, Tiger Rag,* and *Buddy Bolden,* and Mezzrow also had a number of his own called *Really the Blues.* We only played concert dates there but the Frenchmen really enjoyed hearing us play so many of the numbers that until then they had only heard on records. They take our kind of music much more seriously than they do in our own country.

As a leader Mezzrow was a very nice fellow to work for. We didn't have rehearsals because everyone in the outfit knew the numbers. That's why he got that sort of band. We knew what we were going to play and were all thoroughly acquainted with the style of music he wanted.

While abroad I came into contact with quite a few of the European jazz bands. A fellow named Claude Luter has a little band in France and he's got the same instrumentation that King Oliver had. I think they played very well. He plays a lot like my brother because he learned to play by listening to his records. They studied the old records very carefully and tried to get everything down as perfectly as they could. Since they only had the records to teach them they played on the style of our music. Of course on the records they could hear only the cymbals and wood blocks and that is what they mostly used, since they couldn't hear the snares and bass drum as distinctly. They loved my way of drumming because they had heard the records for years and they all seemed so happy to hear me in person.

I was especially glad to find that there was no race prejudice in France, none whatsoever. It was a grand feeling never to come in contact with that. We were in one of the finest hotels in France and never had any difficulty at all. The only thing is, the French do call us black men, which of course we are, so that's nothing to get excited about.

We had loads of fun in France. We were always invited to some dinner party or something and, of course, I had my share of champagne. And every time we went to another place a local band would meet us at the station. They were street bands rather than jazz bands but sometimes they played jazz numbers for us and sometimes patriotic ones. Of course I got to meet some of the jazz fans there including Hugues Panassié. We spent a day in his home in a little suburban town just outside Paris, and he treated us royally. The house was ours. We played in his town and we ate dinner at Panassié's house. His wife even washed a couple of shirts for me. He had every recording that I had made and he played all of them. It made me feel very happy to know that he had these records and to see how much he cherished them.

Our biggest thrill in France was playing at the Nice Festival. It was a very big thing and the best class of people attended it. It was full dress, the ladies were out in their gowns and it was just real "classy." And to be in the midst of such an environment made me feel awfully good. The concerts were held in one of the finest hotels and we were on for an entire week. Ours was just one of the bands. There was also a band from England, and Rex Stewart had an outfit, and Louis Armstrong. Louis had a very good band with Jack Teagarden, Barney Bigard, Big Sid Catlett on drums, Earl Hines on piano and Arvell Shaw on bass. Velma Middleton took some of the vocals with his group. But our band played more on the style which Louis had been used to playing. We had more the New Orleans type of outfit. Our band was especially careful to start sharply and to end the same way, in the New Orleans tradition. Louis liked Mezzrow's band very much and he used to sit and listen carefully while we played. He said it sounded wonderful and even said, "You've got a better band than I have." Well, we knew that was a joke. But in another way it was a reality to him because our way of playing was the style that Louis used to play, and especially my style of drumming. Of course both Pops Foster and I had played with Louis on the riverboats years before, and I guess it just put music in his ears to hear us again.

I returned from Europe in April of 1948 and went back with the Art Hodes trio until about September of the same year. Then I went to Chicago to play at the Beehive with Miff Mole and his band. The group included Miff Mole, who played trombone, a fellow named Gronwall on piano, Darnell Howard on clarinet and a trumpet player named Freddie Greenleaf who was from Detroit. The band as a whole sounded pretty good, and we played all kinds of numbers. That was the place where I signed a year's contract without knowing that it was for so long a period. The owner of the Beehive had sent for me when I was in New York and I just signed the contract without reading half of it, thinking it was for a few weeks or months at the most. Later I was very much surprised to learn that I had signed up for a whole year.

When I got there I also found out that the owner tried to put special conditions on my activities. He said someone had told him that I would drink so much I would get drunk and run everybody out of the place and even beat up the boss. They also told him that I was pretty mean. Of course I couldn't have been in the music business for such a long time if the story had been true. But he tried to put laws on me. I wasn't to drink at the bar. I wasn't supposed to sit with parties. I told him that I would not stay on a job with such a feeling. I would not work for a boss I disliked. I would not work for a boss whom I feared. And furthermore I wouldn't work for a man if I disliked the people who worked for him. I told him I wanted to work at a place where people welcomed me and liked me. Then I could give my best. But if I felt that someone on the job didn't like me I couldn't do my best.

According to my theory of drumming a person must be relaxed. You can't be tense or afraid that you're going to do wrong. Music must be played in a relaxed mood in the first place. You must feel free to do what you want to do. When you do that you're not tightened up in any way. Then you've got clear thoughts as to what you are going to do and what's going to happen. When relaxed you can put your mind to your music and play it right. You can't be worried with other things but you've got to do this one specific thing, with full confidence that you know perfectly well what you want to do, and can do it right.

Later on my boss at the Beehive found out that everything he had been told about me was a bad joke. I was very popular there and many people used to call me over to have a drink. One night I drank steadily all evening. When I didn't get drunk at all it surprised the owner so much that he acknowledged his mistake, and said he wouldn't bother me anymore about my drinking. After that I had no more trouble with him. I used to drink nothing but gin then and I didn't like the Gordon gin he carried because it was too strong. He asked me what kind I would like and when I told him Gilbey's he had some brought in for me. After he found out what I liked he ordered a whole case of gin for me every week. In a week's time I drank up a case. Various people came in and bought me drinks and, of course, he made money on my drinking or he wouldn't have gone to the trouble of having a special brand kept on hand just for me.

Even though my Beehive contract was for a year I didn't stay there for that length of time. In April of 1949 I returned to New York for my car and some other things I had left there and while in New York I had my first stroke. I was very sick but some friends took care of me and I didn't have to go to the hospital. In June I flew back to Chicago and went right to bed. I was in and out of bed, without even being able to sit up for a long period of time. Later, although I still wasn't able to work, I went to New York again and became connected with the Conrad Janis outfit. Even though I couldn't play regularly Conrad asked me if I would come to observe their rehearsals. After a while he asked me to sit in on some numbers and before long I was drumming with the band. We got a job at a jam session and through that we landed an engagement to play in a Philadelphia hotel for several weeks. We had Dick Wellstood, Henry Goodwin, Jimmy Archey, Conrad Janis and myself. I was the only oldtimer in the band and Conrad placed a lot of responsibility in me and it gave me quite a bit of respect. I would show them and they were interested in learning. I told them how the different numbers were supposed to be played, not too fast, and not too slow. It was when I was with Janis that I had my second stroke. That was in 1950 and I was seriously ill in a New York hospital from April until the latter part of May. I had loads of friends who visited me but it was very tough to be confined like that without even being able to take care of myself.

Of course, as soon as I got well enough I wanted to play again and in 1951 I played a series of dances in Chicago with Natty Dominique's outfit. They were sponsored by Bill Russell and Barbara Reid and lasted for several weeks. The outfit consisted of Natty on trumpet, Preston Jackson on trombone, Ralph Tervelon on piano, Odell Rand on clarinet, and me on drums. But I couldn't drum a whole evening at a time so we also had Jasper Taylor to play drums when I felt that I should stop. I had known Jasper ever since I came to Chicago. He did mostly show work but he was a marvelous drummer and one that I would call a finished drummer because he read music very well. The outfit was billed as one that played "slow drag" music. And that was because of me. I just couldn't beat drums fast, and to bring me into it Natty used to play lots of slow numbers. That way I could drum very well. Nobody but Natty Dominique would have done something like that.

Dominique was a very nice leader, too. He wasn't particularly strict because he hired men that knew just what to do. For the same reason he had very few rehearsals. Natty wanted a drummer who would work, not a drummer who drowned anybody out, but one who would play with the band. And when a guy can't do that Dominique feels he can't drum. Well, he's right. If you haven't got a system to your drumming—if you can't play loud when you are supposed to play loud, and soft when you're supposed to play soft—you just aren't much of a drummer. That was a very nice hard-working outfit which Natty had but it didn't go over so well and the dances didn't continue long enough for them to catch on.

I visited New York again in both 1951 and 1952 but, despite my best efforts to play, I just couldn't. I tried to play in jam sessions but my coordination was gone. However, I didn't give up and in 1952, although I wasn't so hot, I did a little better than the year before. Then, too, people didn't want to hire me and take a chance for fear I might get sick again while working for them. In December of 1952 I again went to New York and played with a group of youngsters, the Dixieland Rhythm Kings, at Ryan's Number Two place. I was anxious to play and although they called me up about the job late one night I went out and worked that whole night. Although just a group of youngsters they were conscientious and worked very hard. And that night I was somewhat nervous and drank about five or six drinks of whiskey, and I shouldn't have done that. The next day I had my third stroke. Fortunately, however, I wasn't so sick that I had to go to bed and I was all right again within a few days.

    Although I haven't played with a regular outfit since then I still live for my drums and feel that some day I will come back and play even better than before. I have had all kinds of musical experiences and played with outfits of all sizes and varieties. And I had no preference as to size of band. I liked all of them. I've played for street parades, dancing, shows, radio and recording, and even solos. Some of the bands, like King Oliver's and my brother's, were jazz bands, and some, like Hughie Swift's and Charlie Elgar's, were large dance bands that played more straight music than jazz. I've played with outfits containing all kinds of musical instruments, violins, and mellophone included. One time I even played a dance with just my drums and Jack Carey's trombone and on one regular job I played drums with only Lonnie Johnson's guitar carrying melody. All of these experiences have contributed to my knowledge of drumming and I have thought a great deal about the different music I have heard and helped to make. Lots of ideas have come to me even though I haven't yet been able to execute them. One of my pet ideas is to write and work out a drum symphony, which would involve five or six drummers all carrying out the ideas of one lead drummer. I've done this with one other drummer and I don't see why a group couldn't do the same thing. It's never been done and I don't know where we'd get the group to do it. But it is one of the ideas that I have outlined in my head. I may never work that one out but I am still working at my drums and I feel confident that someday I will again carry out with my drumsticks and drum sets the ideas that I am now carrying around in my head.

Selected Recordings

Long-Playing Records

Because of the compact disc revolution, long-playing records are becoming increasingly difficult to find. Some specialty shops still carry them, and they sometimes appear on lists of used jazz recordings.

The Baby Dodds Trio. GHB 50. Includes Baby Dodds's unique solo drum improvisations as well as his drum backing for a trio and for Don Ewell's piano.

Tony Parenti's Ragtimers and Ragpickers. Jazzology J-15.

Muggsy Spanier and His All-Stars. Jazzology J-33. From the 1947 "This is Jazz" broadcasts.

Art Hodes: The Trios. Jazzology J-113. Includes four selections with Baby Dodds, recorded in 1953 after he had suffered a series of strokes.

Giants of Traditional Jazz. Savoy SJL 2251. A two-record set containing the ten 1947 sides Baby Dodds made with Mutt Carey's band.

King Oliver's Jazz Band, 1923. The Smithsonian Collection R001. Despite the primitive recording techniques, these are important historically and include all of Oliver's Columbia and Okeh recordings. Dodds's presence is mostly felt rather than heard.

Compact Discs

Bunk Johnson, "The King of the Blues." American Music AMCD-1. Bill Russell's American Music recordings from the mid-1940s feature some of

Selected Recordings

Baby Dodds's best work. This is the first of a complete series to be issued by George Buck of New Orleans.

George Lewis with Kid Shots. American Music AMCD-2. Baby Dodds plays drums in all fifteen selections on this disc. "Ice Cream" features some of his greatest drumming.

Bunk Johnson 1944. American Music AMCD-3. More of Baby's well-recorded drumming with Bunk's band.

Johnny Dodds: Blue Clarinet Stomp. Bluebird 2293-2-RB. Has thirteen numbers, 1927–29, with Baby Dodds, including the two trio selections he made with Jelly Roll Morton.

The Centennial Jelly Roll Morton: His Complete Victor Recordings. Bluebird 2361-2-RB. A five-disc set that has twelve of the 1927 Red Hot Peppers tracks with Baby Dodds on drums and two trio numbers, including an alternate take of "Wolverine Blues."

Sidney Bechet: The Victor Sessions, Master Takes 1932–43. Bluebird 2402-2-RB. This three-disc set includes one 1940 track of Baby Dodds with a trio and four with the New Orleans Feetwarmers.

Louis Armstrong: The Hot Fives and Hot Sevens, Vol. II. Columbia CK 44253. Baby Dodds plays drums on all eight of the 1927 Hot Seven numbers.

Louis Armstrong: The Hot Fives and Hot Sevens, Vol. III. Columbia CK 44422. Dodds is on three of the Hot Seven numbers.

Johnny Dodds: South-Side Chicago Jazz. MCA:Decca, MCAD-42326. Has ten selections with various groups featuring Johnny Dodds and Baby Dodds.

Louis Armstrong of New Orleans. MCA:Decca, MCAD 42328. Includes the 1927 "Wild Man Blues" with Baby Dodds.

Additional Reading

Charters, Samuel B. *Jazz: New Orleans, 1885–1957.* Belleville, N.J., 1958. A biographical dictionary of black musicians from New Orleans, including many who worked with or were mentioned by Baby Dodds.

Gara, Larry. "Baby Dodds: Drummer Extraordinary." *Negro History Bulletin* (April, 1954), 151–52, 159.

Hodes, Art, and Chadwick Hansen, eds. *Selections from the Gutter: Portraits from "The Jazz Record."* Berkeley, 1977. Includes "Oh, Play That Thing," a 1946 interview with Baby Dodds, and George Wettling's "Baby Dodds Knew How."

Hoeffer, George, Jr. "Ah, Yes We Know—Baby Dodds." *Hot Record Society Rag* (March, 1941), 2–10.

King, Bruce. "Gigantic Baby Dodds." *Jazz Review* (August, 1960), 12–15.

Ramsey, Frederick, and Charles Edward Smith, eds. *Jazzmen.* 1939; rpr. New York, 1985. Contains chapters on New Orleans music and the King Oliver Creole Jazz Band.

Rose, Al, and Edmond Souchon. *New Orleans Jazz: A Family Album.* Baton Rouge, 3rd ed., 1984. Contains biographical information on many New Orleans contemporaries of Baby Dodds, as well as information on the bands, dance halls, and riverboats.

Russell, William. "Baby Talk." *Jazzbeat* (Spring, 1990), 10–11. An interview with Baby Dodds made in 1953.

Schafer, William J., with Richard B. Allen. *Brass Bands and New Orleans*

Jazz. Baton Rouge, 1977. Packed with information about the early New Orleans brass bands that formed a part of Baby Dodds's musical education.

Shapiro, Nat, and Nat Hentoff, eds. *Hear Me Talkin' to Ya: The Story of Jazz by the Men Who Made It.* 1955; rpr. New York, 1966. Includes material by and about Baby Dodds.

———. *The Jazz Makers.* 1957; rpr. Westport, Conn., 1975. Contains an excellent chapter on Baby Dodds by Nat Hentoff.

Thompson, Kay C. "Baby Dodds in the Role of Critical Listener." *Jazz Journal* (March, 1951), 1–2.

———. "Baby Dodds in the Role of Music Coach." *Jazz Journal* (April, 1950), 1–2.

Wettling, George. "A Tribute to Baby Dodds." *Downbeat,* March 29, 1962, p. 21.

Williams, Martin. *Jazz Masters of New Orleans.* 1967; rpr. New York, 1979. Has information about the Dodds brothers as well as other New Orleans musicians of their time.

Index

Ace in the Hole, 11, 29
Albert's Blues, 77
Alexander, Charlie, 50
American Stars band, 9, 11, 16, 18
Anchors Aweigh, 53
Anderson, Bill, 86
Archey, Jimmy, 91, 94
Armstrong, Lillian Hardin, 34, 45-46, 65, 69, 70, 72
Armstrong, Louis, 21, 22, 24, 25-26, 31-32, 35, 38, 40, 46, 67, 70, 74, 79, 81, 92-93; and his Hot Seven, 72-73

Baquet, George, 12
Barbarin, Paul, 48
Barker, Danny, 81
Barrett, Emma, 19
Bates, Frank, 51
Bauduc, Ray, 27, 63-64
Bechet, Sidney, 14; and his New Orleans Feetwarmers, 76
Beehive, The, 93
Beer, Sam, 55, 56
Beiderbecke, Bix, 24
Benskin, Sammy, 77
Berle, Milton, 89
Bertrand, Jimmy, 67
"Big Eye Lil," 52
Bigard, Barney, 49, 92
Billy Goat Stomp, 74
Bishop, Wally, 64
"Black Benny," 8
Blesh, Rudi, 77, 79, 80-82
Blues, 11, 20, 29-30
Blues For You, Johnny, 76
Blythe, Jimmy, 70-71

Bolden, Buddy, 12, 17
Bontemps, Willie, 19, 64
Boogie woogie, 56
Braud, Wellman, 77
Brown, Boyce, 62
Brown, Cleo, 55-56
Brown, Ralph, 65
Brundy, Walter, 7, 27-28, 39
Brunies, George, 62, 81
Buddy Bolden's Blues, 78, 91
Bucket Got a Hole In It, 11
Bushell, Garvin, 77
Butterfield, Billy, 63

California Theatre, 34
Callahan's Bar, 58-59
Campbell, Arthur, 57
Canadian Capers, 33
Canal Street Blues, 70
Capitol (riverboat), 21
Capone, Al, 58
Careless Love, 11
Carey, Jack, 13-14, 18, 96
Carey, Mutt, 14, 18, 34; and his New Yorkers, 82-83
Carnegie Hall, 89
Casino (Villa Cafe), 11
Catlett, Big Sid, 92
Celestin, Oscar "Sonny," 18, 19-20, 21
Chauffeur's Club, 31
Chicago Opera House, 75
Christian, ..., 67
Clarence Black's Band, 67
Club Bagdad, 65
Cobb, Bert, 49
Cohen, Mrs. ...., 59
Collins, Lee, 77

101

Index

Condon, Eddie, 63, 89
Congress Casino, 61, 86
Cottrell, Louis, 7, 8
Creath, Charlie, 31
Creole musicians, 13
Crosby, Bob, 61, 63
Crystal, Jack, 89
Cunningham, Merce, 90-91

Dardanella, 51
Davenport, Iowa, 21, 24, 28
Davison, Wild Bill, 63, 81
Decou, Walter, 10
de Pass, Arnold, 85
Desvigne, Sidney, 10
Didn't He Ramble, 17
Dille, Sheelagh, 78
Dinah, 61, 86
Dippermouth Blues, 36, 39, 69-70
Dixieland Rhythm Kings, 83, 95-96
Dixieland Thumpers, 71
Dodds, Irene (Mrs. Warren), 47
Dodds, Johnny, 2, 3-4, 11, 14-15, 18, 21, 38, 40, 44, 49, 50-55, 56, 57-63, 68, 70-76, 96
Dodds, Warren "Baby," early family life, 1-5; first drum set, 5-6; studies in New Orleans, 6-9; with American Stars Band, 9, 11; with Eagle Band, 16; with Sonny Celestin's band, 19-20; with Fate Marable band, 21-32; with Oliver band, 33-48; first marriage, 34; second marriage, 47; with Johnny Dodds' outfits, 50-55, 57-62; with Hughie Swift Band, 66-67; with Charlie Elgar Band, 67; records with Oliver band, 69-70; records with Armstrong's Hot Seven, 72-73; records with Johnny's outfit, 70-72, 75-76; records with Jelly Roll Morton's Red Hot Peppers, 73-75; later recordings, 76-84; broadcasting, 80-82; drum solos, 83-84; with Bunk Johnson's band, 87-89; free lance work, 55-56, 65-68, 85-86, 89-90, 93-96; in Europe, 91-93; drum techniques, 26-27, 38-39, 56-57, 86-87, 88, 90-91
Dodds, William, 60
Do Right Baby, 79n
Dominique, Natty, 51, 53, 56, 57, 58, 59, 60, 61, 68, 70, 75, 76, 88, 95
Downbeat Club, 56
Downes, Ormand, 63

Drake Hotel, 46
Dreamland, 65
Drum techniques, 26-27, 38-39, 56-57, 86-87, 88, 90-91
Drums, importance in band, 11-12, 39
Dubuque, Iowa, 21
Duson, Frankie, 12, 13, 16, 18, 20
Dutrey, Honoré, 19, 34, 38, 43-44, 50, 60, 70
Dutrey, Pete, 60
Dutrey, Sam, 24, 60

Eagle Band, 16, 18
Eclipse Alley Five, 79
Eldridge, Roy, 55
Elgar, Charles, 51, 67, 96
Evergreen Golf Club, 66
Ewell, Don, 77-78

Faust, 59
Fewclothes Cafe, 9
Foster, George "Pops," 14-15, 21, 78, 80, 81, 89, 91, 93
Frankie and Johnny, 29
Freeman, Bud, 37, 63
Fresno, California, 34
Funerals, in New Orleans, 17-18

Gallo, Rocco, 58
Garland, Eddie, 15, 34, 35
Godchaux Building, 79
Gonsoulin, Bertha, 35
Goodman, Benny, 37, 65
Goodwin, Henry, 89, 91, 94
Granada, 38, 80
Gravier Street Blues, 76
Greenleaf, Freddie, 93
Gronwall, ___, 93
Gully Low, 36

Haggart, Bobby, 63
Hampton, Lionel, 65
Hall, Edmond, 77, 81
Hall, Minor, 8, 33
Hall, Tubby, 8, 76
Hannibal, Missouri, 28-29
Hardin, Lillian, see Armstrong, Lillian
Henderson, Fletcher, 36
Hiawatha, 82
High Society, 10, 34, 91
Hightower, Willie, 9, 11, 65
Hill, Bertha "Chippie," 61, 76, 77, 81
Hines, Earl, 76, 92

Index

Hodes, Art, 63, 77, 78, 87, 89, 93
Holliday, Billie, 55
Hotel Sherman, 86
Howard, Darnell, 49, 56, 93
Howard, Joe, 24
Hungarian Rhapsodies, 59
Hyena Stomp, 74

Improvisation Number Two, 83-84
In the Shade of the Old Apple Tree, 10
Irish Channel, New Orleans, 13

J.S., (riverboat), 21, 27
Jack Sheehan's Roadhouse, 19
Jackson, Dewey, 31
Jackson, Eddie, 12
Jackson, Preston, 44, 75, 76, 95
Jackson, Tony, 12
Janis, Conrad, 94
Jazzland, 31
Jeffrey Tavern, 66, 80
Jeffries, Herb, 55, 76
Johnson, Bill, 40, 50-51, 70
Johnson, Ed "Noon," 79n
Johnson, James P., 81, 89
Johnson, Joe, 12
Johnson, Lonnie, 56, 75, 96
Johnson, Odell, 34
Johnson, Willie G. "Bunk," 7, 16, 60, 78-80, 87-89
Jones, Clifford, 48
Jones, David, 24, 33-34, 35
Jones, King, 42, 58
Jones, Richard M. "Myknee," 75, 76
Joplin, Scott, 10
Jungle Blues, 74

K-Nine Club, 59, 63-65, 67
Kaminsky, Max, 89
Kapp, Jack, 71
Kelly, Burt, 50-52
Kelly's Stables, 50-52, 55, 61, 63, 89
Keokuk, Iowa, 21, 22
Keppard, Freddie, 50, 52, 60
Kimball, Andrew, 12
Krupa, Gene, 63, 64, 65, 87

LaCrosse, Wisconsin, 21
Ladnier, Tommy, 63
Lamare, Nappy, 63
Lamb's Club, 57-58
Laroque, George, 12
Laugh, Clown, Laugh, 30
Lawson, Yank, 63

Lee, Julia, 56
Lewis, George, 60, 79, 87
Lim, Harry, 86
Lincoln Gardens, 35-44, 58, 59, 63, 64, 65, 70
Lincoln Park, New Orleans, 12
Lindsay, Johnny, 75, 76
Lion, Alfred, 77
Listen to Me, 79
Liza Jane, 20
Lombardo, Guy, 80
Lower Deck, The, 58
Ludwig, William, 27
Lugg, George, 89
Luter, Claude, 91

McCurdy, Charlie, 14
McKendrick, Mike, 66, 79, 80
McMurray, ..., 6-7
McPartland, Jimmy, 63
Major, Miss ...., 45
Maltz, Bob, 89
Manetta, Manuel, 11
Manhattan Stomp, 78
Maple Leaf Rag, 34, 89
Marable, Fate, 20, 22, 23-26, 28-29, 31
Mares, Paul, jam sessions, 61-63
Marrero, Billy, 78
Marrero, Lawrence, 78, 79, 87
Martin, Henry, 8, 15, 19
Memphis Blues, 11
Memphis, Tennessee, 49
Mente's bag factory, 5-6
Mezzrow, Milton "Mezz," 63, 76, 91
Middleton, Velma, 92
Midway Gardens, 66
Missouri Waltz, 80
Mole, Miff, 28, 93
Montgomery, Leo, 57, 58, 59, 61, 68
Montudie, see Garland, Eddie
Moore, Freddie, 81
Morton, Jelly Roll, 12, 65, 77; and his Red Hot Peppers, 73-75
Mumford, Brock, 13
Muse, Red, 31
Muskrat Ramble, 91

Narcotics, use of by musicians, 43
Negro musicians, attitude toward, 28, 34, 61-62; influence on white jazz, 61-65
Nelson, Big Eye Louis, 12-13
Nervebeats, 84
New Orleans, 34, 56, 64, 76, 79, 85,

Index

86; classical music in, 3; jazz in, 10-11, 12-14, 15-19, 61-62; blues in, 29-30
——————— street parades, 16-19
——————— funerals, 17-18
——————— tradition in jazz, 36-37
New Plantation, 49, 58
New Stables, 59, 65
New York, jazz in, 87-90
New York Herald Tribune, 79
Nice, France, 91, 92
Nicholas, Albert, 49, 77, 81
Nichols, Red, 28
Nick's, 89
9750 Club, 67
Noone, Jimmie, 76, 85-86

Oakland, California, 35
O'Brien, Floyd, 62
O'Day, Anita, 55
O'Hare, Husk, 44, 66
Oliver, Joe "King," 18, 20, 33, 38, 44, 48-49, 64, 69, 70, 91, 96
——————— King Oliver Band, 32, 47-48, 50, 59; in San Francisco, 33-35; at Lincoln Gardens, 35-44; recording sessions, 69-70
Oppenheimer, ..., 59
Ory, Edward "Kid," 8, 11, 14-15, 16, 18, 21, 34, 49, 65
Over the Waves, 10, 66

Palao, Jimmy, 34, 35
Palmer, 9, 10, 66
Panama, 61, 91
Panassie, Hugues, 92
Paps, ... "Rabbit," 8
Parades, in New Orleans, 16-19
Parenti, Tony, and his Ragtimers, 82
Paris, France, 91
Pavageau, Alcide "Slow Drag," 60, 79, 87
Pencil Papa, 36
Perez, Manuel, 60
Pergola Dance Hall, 34
Perkins, Dave, 7
Petit, Buddy, 12
Picou, Alphonse, 10, 12
Piron, Armand, 8
Plantation, The, 48-49
Play, Jack Carey, 14
Point a la Hache, Louisiana, 88
Pollack, Ben, 37, 63-64
"Pork Chops," 57
Praline, 82

President (riverboat), 21
Price, Sammy, 91

Quadback, Al, 58

Ragtime, 10
Rainey, Ma, 8, 30
Rand, Odell, 95
Raye, Martha, 55
Really the Blues, 91
Reed, Fred, 56
Red Onion Blues, 76
Red Wing, Minnesota, 21
Reid, Barbara, 95
Rent parties, 60-61
Ridgley, Bebé, 19
Richmond, Indiana, 69-70
Riverboats, 22-24, 28-29
Riverside Blues, 36, 70
Robichaux, John, 6, 7, 12
Robinson, Jim, 79, 87
Rogers, Buddy, 64
Rolling bass piano style, 56, 61
Roy, Mada, 86
Royal Gardens, 35
Rucker, Laura, 86
Rudiments, 84
Russell, Pee Wee, 63, 65, 89
Russell, William, 78-80, 87, 95
Ryan's, 87, 89
——————— Number Two, 95

St. Catherine's Hall, 11
St. Cyr, Johnny, 13, 60
St. Louis Blues, 11
St. Louis, Missouri, 22, 30-31
St. Paul (riverboat), 21, 27
St. Paul, Minnesota, 21
San Francisco, 33-35
San Jose, California, 34
Santa Cruz, California, 34
Savoy Ballroom, 67
Schoffner, Bob, 49
Scott, Bud, 49, 65
Scott, Cecil, 87, 89
Shaw, Arvell, 92
Shayne, Freddy, 76, 77
Sidney (riverboat), 21, 64
Simms, Arthur, 65
Singleton, Zutty, 61, 64, 67
Smith, Bessie, 30
Smith, Leonard, 65
Smith, Mamie, 30
Smith, Ray, 66, 80
Smith, Robert, 9

Index

Smith, Stuff, 56
Snake Rag, 36, 70
Sobbin' Blues, 70
Someday Sweetheart, 36, 70
Soper, Tut, 76
Spanier, Muggsy, 81, 89
Spooky Drums, 84
Stacy, Jess, 37, 63
Stall, Lorenzo, 13
Steiner, John, 76
Stewart, Rex, 76, 92
Streckfus, ..., 23, 27, 28, 31
——— riverboat line, 21
Stuyvesant Casino, 80, 88
"Sugar Boy," 61
"Sugar Johnny," 86
Sugarfoot Stomp, 36
Sullivan, Joe, 89; benefit for, 61
Swift, Hugh, 66-67, 79, 80, 96
Syncopation, 10

Tate, Erskine, 67
Taylor, Jasper, 95
Tea for Two, 86
Teagarden, Charles, 62
Teagarden, Jack, 62, 92
Tervalon, Ralph, 60, 95
Teschemacher, Frank, 37, 65
That's a Plenty, 62
"This is Jazz" (radio program), 80-82
Thompson, Kay, 64-65
Three Deuces, 55, 64
Tiger Rag, 14, 34, 61-62, 91
Tin Pan Alley, 86

Tio, Lorenzo "Papa," 14, 19-20
Todd, Sterling, 58
Tom-Tom Workout, 84
Tough, Dave, 37, 63
Trepagnier, Ernest, 17
Tulane Theatre, 3
29 Club, 58

Villa Cafe, 11
Village Vanguard, 77

Wahl, Archie, 65
Waller, Fats, 55
Washington, Sister Ernestine, 80
Waters, Herb, 57, 59
Waters of Minnetonka, 66, 80
Waveland, Mississippi, 5
Wellstood, Dick, 94
Wettling, George, 37, 63
Whaley, Wade, 9, 14, 34
When the Saints Go Marching In, 87
Whiteman, Paul, 37-38
Wilbur, Bob, 91
Williams, Clarence, 89
Willie the Weeper, 72-73
Wilson, Teddy, 65
Wolverine Blues, 77
Wynn, Al, 44, 65

Yancey, Jimmy, 61
Yancey, Mama, 61

Zeno, Henry, 8, 16
Zurke, Bob, 63